They Called My Name

Donald J. Metz

BOOKS

Copyright © 2023 by Donald J. Metz

All rights reserved

No part of this publication may be reproduced, distributed, or transmitted in any form or by any means, including photocopying, recording, or other electronic or mechanical methods, without the prior written permission of the publisher, except as permitted by copyright law.

ISBN 978-0-9950623-2-0 (book)
ISBN 978-0-9950623-4-4 (hardcover book)
ISBN 978-0-9950623-3-7 (ebook)

Photo Credits
Front/Back cover: Jody Thoen
All other photos by author
Lyrics to Grandfather courtesy Winston Wuttenee

Published by IDA BOOKS
Salmon Arm, B.C.
Canada

For Jason, Zach, Zuri, Monroe, and Bjorn

They Called My Name

Contents

———————

Preface	vii

CHAPTERS

1.	Two Days in Carignan	1
2.	Napoleon's Curse	14
3.	No Place For Us	31
4.	A New Age	44
5.	Society as Donald enters the World	64
6.	Navigating The Teen Years	83
7.	The March To War	99
8.	England	118
9.	The Raid on Frankfurt	137
10.	La Terre Rouge	156
11.	My Journey	171
12.	Carignan	182
13.	War, What Is It Good For?	196

Acknowledgements	219

Preface

At some point in our lives, most of us ruminate about our names. How do parents choose to name their children? Often, a stream of popular names emanates from celebrities and sports stars. Other times a book of names is the source, explaining the origins, meanings, and ethnic variations of a list of names. Sometimes we change our names, and other times they are a source of comedy or endless ridicule. If John Hardy marries Jane Harr, will they have a Hardy-Harr wedding? In his poem "What's in a Name?" Simon Gowen calls for a plumber named Lee King and cites a coast guard ship's mate named Aaron C. Reskew. I never had a daughter, but if I did, her name would have been Amanda Lynn.

For others, tradition is the motivation behind the choice of our name. In many families, certain names are common throughout their genealogy, and in some cases our names are given to honour another person. In my case, I was given the name of an uncle who joined the Canadian Air Force at the age of nineteen and died on his first mission in World War II.

I initially became aware of my namesake when his name was called at a Remembrance Day service. I wanted to know: why did they call my name? My uncle died long before I was able to meet him and come to know him. Simply knowing that my name came from my uncle was not satisfying. He gave his life so I could live mine in peace. I wanted to know much more about him, and my curiosity led me on a lifelong journey to understand who he was, where he came from, and how the world he grew up in compared to the world I knew.

Most people would consider a book of this nature to be a labour of love, and indeed it has been. However, I believe that in our world today – considering the rise of populism, the Russian invasion of Ukraine, and Trumpism in the USA – there is a greater need for understanding the freedoms we enjoy and how we can preserve them for our children.

Chapter 1

Two Days in Carignan

The two most important days in your life are the day you are born and the day you find out why.

— Mark Twain[1]

November 26, 1943

Stanislas stirred in his sleep, awakened by a penetrating roar in the dead of night. He sprang from his bed, hurried to the window, and stared into the evening solitude. The thin, waxing crescent of a new moon was barely visible. As Stanislas' eyes adapted to the darkness, he could see a few distant, dimly lit stars piercing the murky skies. He looked for a moment into a landscape he knew well and concentrated on the echoes of the night. He thought he had heard the faint rumblings of an engine in the distance, a plane he assumed was flying at a low altitude.

Suddenly, there was a powerful yet muffled explosion in the distance, then a deadly calm. His ears strained, but the disturbance in the far off darkness diminished as quickly as it appeared. Stanislas lingered vigilant and silent, contemplative yet curious. He thought to himself, *I must discover what happened.* The young Stanislas Zdeb, barely fourteen years old on the early morning of November 26, 1943, shuffled back to bed and crawled under the covers, unable to return to sleep. He lay restless, reflecting on the war: he was too young to serve his country yet too old to discount the consequences.

Although barely a teenager, Stanislas was not unfamiliar with the war. In an effort to impede invading forces from Germany, the French government had built the Maginot Line, which passed through the Ardennes region of France near Stanislas' home in Osnes.[2] While the line was generally poorly fortified in the region, Stanislas was familiar, since early childhood, with the concrete fortifications and the armoured cloches a few kilometers away. In French, the term *cloche* translates to *bell*, which described the shape of many of these structures. Almost two hundred cloches dotted the Maginot Line alongside the French border with Germany, Luxembourg, and Belgium. A cloche was only about the size of a backyard tool shed, but they stood in harsh contrast against the serene and picturesque French countryside.

Stanislas was not unfamiliar with the wailing sounds of the German *Luftwaffe* cruising overhead and the clamour of the military vehicles advancing by his home to control the French countryside. One of the major battles of the war was for the town of Sedan, twenty kilometers to the east of the Zdeb household, on the banks of the Meuse River. In the invasion of 1940, the Germans captured the town and seized control of the bridges crossing the river, advancing through the vulnerable French countryside to the English Channel. The British expeditionary forces were driven from the continent, and the French army was defeated, allowing Germany to occupy France.

Young Stanislas' memory of the battle of Sedan remained vivid. The rumbling of the Panzer tanks as they rolled by, the artillery fire, and the panic and terror of civilians were impressions that would remain with him forever. The town of Sedan had been evacuated, and many of the residents fled along the roads by his home. However, tonight was different. The German forces now occupied the region, and members of the French resistance had receded underground. What did the explosion signal? Stanislas wondered if it would be another bombing raid, a new invasion, or an accidental crash. He thought to himself, *what else could it be?* "Soon we'll see," he whispered as he lay back in his bed, no longer able to sleep.

Many other residents in the vicinity also heard the crash, and the word quickly spread through town. A young woman, Mme Berriot,[3] also heard the thunder of the impending crash and immediately went outside to find the location. Berriot was a female member of the *Maquis*, the French resistance. During the war, women could often move about more freely than the men. They showed great bravery while helping with the resistance, especially with downed aviators.

Seeing the flames on a nearby hill, Berriot advanced quickly to attend the scene. She was the first person who approached the plane that crashed on Mount Tilleul, just outside of the town of Carignan. About a half kilometer from the burning plane, Berriot ran into a young man, slightly over six feet tall with light brown hair. The young man, disoriented and in a state of confusion, was hastily walking away from the scene. His hair was burned, his face blackened with oil and soot. He wore a long trench coat and a pair of Irving trousers. Mme Berriot cleaned his face with her handkerchief and removed the Irving trousers, which she later hid in the nearby cemetery. The crash survivor was wearing blue-grey battledress jeans under his Irvings, and he refused further help. They both knew the Gestapo would soon be arriving to investigate and arrest anyone in the area. The young man spoke some French, but very poorly, and he asked which direction was Belgium. Berriot pointed him towards the border, and the wounded aviator hurriedly made off in that direction. Mme Berriot then quickly fled back to town, and the next day she burned the Irving trousers she had hidden in the cemetery.

As the early morning arrived, Stanislas could not sleep, so he devoured his breakfast and bolted out the door from his home in Osnes before dawn. He met a friend down the road who was also aroused by the explosion, and they made their way towards the nearby village of Carignan. They could walk there in about half an hour, and as the cold day appeared, they hurried along the road. The boys met others on the way and learned that a plane had crashed near the Linden tree on Mount Tilleul, close by Carignan. As they approached the hill nearby, the Gestapo suddenly appeared and warned them to retreat. The crowd scattered, and Stanislas and his companion hid in some nearby bushes where they could see the wreckage of the downed plane. The boys saw some men lying motionless in the debris, and they could see pieces of their uniforms on a few of the bodies. The other occupants were burned and mutilated beyond recognition. The Mayor of Carignan, Monsieur Colle, arrived and hurriedly removed the bodies of the airmen, placing them in wooden coffins. He mounted the coffins on a cart pulled by two oxen and descended the hill towards the cemetery. Some townsfolk waited at the bottom of the hill nearby the cemetery. They held bouquets of remembrance, but the Gestapo had arrived at the same time, guns drawn, terrifying the crowd and scaring them away. Stanislas remembered:

The Gestapo that arrived at the same time prevented people from approaching with flowers, threatening them, weapons in hand. Mayor Colle urged us to leave knowing that the Germans were in danger of shooting at us.[4]

At the cemetery, chaos ensued. The town's mayor, knowing the Germans were capable of firing at anyone, yelled at young Stanislas and his friends, and he motioned vigorously for them to leave the area. They hurriedly fled to the houses in the neighbourhood. Some men swiftly dug four pits and placed the remains of the aviators in the graves; three in one, two in another, and one in each of the remaining two graves. The coffins were covered with earth. When the Germans left, Stanislas returned to the cemetery to see where the men had been buried. From that day on, Mount Tilleul became known as *La Terre Rouge* (The Red Earth) by the local citizenry. The men were laid to rest; their war was over.[5]

* * *

April 24, 2013

I stood by serenely, reflecting on my surroundings, looking at my name on the gravestone. The inscription read D.J. Metz, died November 26, 1943, age nineteen. My name was carved in stone, but the grave was not mine. My companions, the deputy mayor of the town of Carignan, members of the local historical society, the English teacher from the town's high school and her husband, and my good friend Pierre Lauginie from Paris, remained quietly nearby, granting me a few moments of silence. I glanced briefly beyond the solemn gateway to the cemetery beside the rolling country hills, dressed brilliantly green in

"May His Soul And All The Souls Of The Faithful Departed Rest In Peace."

nature's splendour. The deputy mayor, following my gaze, asked, "Would you like to visit the crash site?"

Like many other Canadian children of the post-World War II baby boom, I was named after my uncle who fulfilled the ultimate sacrifice serving his country in Europe. He was an air gunner in a Halifax bomber that was shot down and crashed on the hillside near Carignan on November 26, 1943. Seventy years had passed since that time, and I was finally able to lay my hand on his resting place and give my thanks. My voyage was initiated long ago by the curiosity of a young boy carrying someone else's name. This lengthy trek in time and space was punctuated by a scarcity of information, and often interrupted by my life's challenges and abundant adventures. As I stood there contemplating my role in this moment, it was clear to me that even though I had arrived at my destination, my journey was not complete.

War is curious. Not in the sense that it is something to admire, but in the sense of making meaning out of it. We repeat the exercise routinely, even though it wreaks havoc on one generation while the next often flourishes. For one D.J. Metz, war meant he was dropping bombs on his ancestral home without questioning, and giving up his life after only nineteen years. For another D.J. Metz, it meant singing with Country Joe and the Fish, "one, two, three, four, what are we fighting for?" Despite their inherent differences, these two disparate human beings carried the same name, and over a lifetime, my ardent curiosity never subsided. I needed to know more about the person whose name I carried.

Standing alongside the gravestone that displayed my name, I wondered what is in a name, anyway. According to a common cliché, "That which we call a rose by any other name would smell as sweet." The implication being that a name should not matter. However, the original phrase, from Shakespeare's classic play *Romeo and Juliet*, is often misinterpreted. In reference to the family feud between the Montagues and Capulets that keeps these lovers apart, Shakespeare's Juliette sighs:

It's only your name that's my enemy. You'd still be yourself even if you stopped being a Montague. What's a Montague anyway?

It isn't a hand, a foot, an arm, a face, or any other part of a man. Oh, be some other name! What does a name mean? The thing we call a rose would smell just as sweet if we called it by any other name.

Names are not merely arbitrary. For Juliette, it was the conflict behind "who is a Montague" and "who is a Capulet" that stood in the way of their love, not who they really were as two people in love. In other words, we must not cling to a name as a label; we must strive to understand what lies beneath the surface. In my life, my uncle's name was merely a label. Now I needed to claw beneath the surface in order to reveal his true self, and in turn, my true self.

If our names are indeed more than just labels, how are they connected to our identities? When parents decide on their baby's name they begin, perhaps for the first time, to reflect on their child's identity. In some cases, parents look to make their child's name unique and distinct from others. In other cases, such as mine, parents choose to name their child after another person, often a family member. We pass on these family traditions with immense pride. A kinfolk's name is given to a child to honour the achievements of a family member, often because of a sacrifice made to their country in a war. For the parents, the loved one's memory lives on with their offspring. For the child, the name they carry embraces a curiosity of their being.

All of us expend much more time and energy than we realize in coming to terms with our names. Michael Hendrick points out that the name you carry "is a crucial factor in developing your sense of self,"[6] and consequently your "sense of self" guides you through various paths of your life and career. As children, we begin a process of fostering our identity early as we struggle with the understanding of who we are and who we want to be. It is a basic human condition to strive to be accepted by others, so we cultivate our being to be accepted by others. Whether that means the cool kids, the jocks, or the brainiacs, we continually try to satisfy our need for belonging.

Psychologists have conducted many examinations into the connections between a person's name and their identity. In his studies, Joubert[7] states that the effects of our given names cover a wide array of issues. We may possess a general preference for personal names, or a like or dislike of one's own given names. There always exists unusual names, stereotypes around names, and naming consequences, such as assigning gender-appropriate or gender-inappropriate names.

Joubert also cites the effects of being named for someone else, nicknaming, and the presentation of oneself through personal names. There is no shortage of the influences our names have on a multitude of matters in our lives. I carried my uncle's name with me my whole life. As I tried to connect my name with my identity, I could not ignore the significance his being would have on me.

Certainly, most of us are familiar with some of the impact our names invite and some of the influence they have on other individuals. A name can be used to mark our social status – good or bad – or it can be used as a burning insult. Sometimes we are labelled by others because of our ethnicity, appearance, language, religion, or sexual preferences. These "tags" can characterize – or mock – the way we express ourselves. They can also affect the way we dress ourselves and they can influence our interests and ignorances.

The various formations of our name convey different meanings. I have been called Don, Donald, Donnie, D. J., Metzie, and of course the ubiquitous *Hey You!* When those names did not fit, others provided "monikers" for me, such as Peewee, Henry, and several more that cannot be mentioned. Each one had its own unique story; in some cases a compliment, in others an affront.

Our given name, and the names we are called, contribute to the development of our character and identity. In coming to terms with my identity through the name I carried, I came to accept that there is an expansive connection between that name and the person who first held it. As a young child, I first made this connection when I heard my name called out at a memorial service on Remembrance Day. Hearing what I thought was my name set in motion a lifetime ambition of getting to know my namesake, and in turn myself. What were his likes and dislikes? What were his ambitions and dreams? His relationships? What was his favourite song? What was the world like when he was my age? The list went on and on.

My goal to understand the person who gave me his name led me to a remarkable predicament; how do you get to know someone whom you can never meet? I could not ask my uncle any questions, or observe and be annoyed by his habits, such as your stereotypical drunk uncle. I couldn't climb on his knee or play catch with him. I had to look outwards for some guidance on how to step into his life.

Stepping into his life reminded me of another memorable phrase, "*Walk a mile in their shoes*". This idiom encourages one to understand the life of another by following their life's path and exploring their experiences, thoughts, and challenges. The phrase is a derivation of the Mary T. Lathrap poem "Judge Softly," published in 1895.

> *Pray, don't find fault with the man that limps,*
> *Or stumbles along the road.*
> *Unless you have worn the moccasins he wears,*
> *Or stumbled beneath the same load.*

The message is that before you falsely judge someone, you must empathize with their life's journey by relating to their life experiences as closely as possible. As Lathrap explains later in the poem:

> *Just for a moment, slip into his mind and traditions*
> *And see the world through his spirit and eyes.*

On this warm, friendly day, as I stood by my namesake's resting place, I wondered how I could slip into my uncle's mind and traditions and see through his eyes when he was forever gone. For me, "walk a mile in his shoes" meant I had to come to understand his entire life, appreciate his heritage, his family, the culture in which he was raised, and how it affected him. I had to live with him, play with him, drink with him, laugh and cry with him, go to school with him, fly the plane with him, and follow him to his final resting place. In order to walk that mile with a genuine understanding, especially the last mile, I had to find experiences that we shared but never knew we had in common.

A short while later, as I reflected on my uncle's nature while standing on the hillside where his plane had crashed, I wondered how the world in which he lived helped shape his life. How could I relate the world he knew with the world I live in? Did we share similar experiences? How could I use these experiences to appreciate his identity, and how did it relate to mine? Attention is often given to a nature versus nurture discussion that examines the extent to which our being is a result of inherited (genetic) or acquired (learned) effects. I came to believe it wasn't one or the other, but the interaction between the two that should drive my quest. In this sense, the focus of my examination became our heritage, upbringing, and life experiences; the influence of our close family members; and especially the context of the world in which we lived. This complex tapestry of culture and heritage, family and friends, and the stories of others who struggled with similar challenges, established a base for my reconciliation. I searched for common threads hidden within these narratives; this awareness led me on a pathway to examine the character and personality of my uncle, and in turn, yielded a rendering of my own true identity.

These stories were crucial. Our culture and heritage, and the intricacies of our relationships in life, reveal not only how others see us but how we view ourselves. As I strolled down the hillside where my uncle lost his life, *La Terre Rouge*, I began to realize how much war had permeated the lives of Donald and his family, and ultimately, me. I soon discovered it was not just the Second World War; it all began more than a century ago with the infamous Napoleon and his conflicts with European powers.

Footnotes Chapter 1

[1] Twain is one of my favourite artists. However, there are many witticisms associated with Mark Twain that he may not have been the first to espouse. For some interesting discussion on Twain visit The Apocryphal Twain, Center for Mark Twain Studies:
https://marktwainstudies.com/tag/the-apocryphal-twain

[2] The town of Osnes is located in the township of Carignan, part of the French district of Sedan, near the Belgian border.

Footnotes cont'd

[3] B. Aptroot, "No. 1 Missing Research and Enquiry Unit, British Forces in France," November 20, 1946.

[4] Stanislas Zdeb, "An eyewitness account of the crash scene on November 26, 1943", *L'union-L'Ardennais, Mis à jour le April 28, 2010,* translation by author.

[5] Members of the 429 Squadron who perished on November 26, 1943, near Carignan, France, are Willys Roland Bloch, Earl Allen Burton, Donald Allan Hogg, Peter Thompson McCallum, Victor Wallace McGray, Donald James Metz, and Timothy Wainwright.

[6] M. Hendrick, "How our names shape our identity," *The Week*, September 15, 2013, https://theweek.com/articles/460056/how-names-shape-identity.

[7] C.E. Joubert, "Personal Names as a Psychological Variable," *Psychological Reports*, (December 1993): 1123.

Chapter 2

Napoleon's Curse

Until you spread your wings, you'll have no idea how far you can fly.

– Napoleon

In the spring of 1813, young Margaretha Gross, peeking out from the window of her modest home, was dismayed at the bloodied refugees marching through her village. Just six years of age, Margaretha was living in the tiny Prussian village of Schierschwende. Prussia was the 18th and 19th century kingdom of Germany, and included, at different times, the regions of Germany, Russia, Poland, Czechoslovakia, Lithuania, Denmark, and Belgium.

A few kilometers away from Margaretha's home was the town of Eisenach, and a short distance further was the city of Erfurt. Today, Erfurt is the capital of the state of Thuringia in central Germany, about three hundred kilometers southwest of Berlin. The area is a picturesque region of rolling hills and fertile plains. Martin Luther had studied in Eisenach and attended the University of Erfurt two centuries earlier. The commitment to a religious life was long standing among the area's residents.

Eisenach was also well-known as the home village of Johann Sebastian Bach, who was born there on March 21, 1685. Another well-known composer, Johann Pachelbel, was an organist in Eisenach's church for a brief time in the 17th century. Pachelbel later moved to Erfurt, where he lived for twelve years. Erfurt was possibly where he wrote his *Canon in D*, popularly known today as a wedding song. The area was a peaceful region with a religious passion, and one can discern the gentle certainty in the repetition of the Canon's melody that these characteristics would be passed on to successive generations.

Margaretha struggled to comprehend the heartrending scene of people fleeing their homes in the Erfurt region of Prussia as Napoleon and his army advanced through the valley at this time. How can we expect a child to comprehend war, or the cravings of military leaders to control and conquer? Children, especially young ones raised in a deeply pious manner, would surely relive these memories throughout their lives.

Europe in the late 18th and early 19th centuries was in an endless state of turmoil and war. During the French revolution the ruling monarchy was overthrown, leading to radical social and political transformations. As part of this political revolution, the emerging republic endured decades of conflict, embodied by the dictatorship and wars of Napoleon Bonaparte. The iconic image of a diminutive Napoleon as he rode his stallion is still fixated in our memories as a distant vestige of this past. Yet Napoleon's impact, and the despair he spread, can still be traced to our lives today.

Bonaparte was born and spent his early life on the island of Corsica in the Mediterranean Sea. Ironically, he was also named after his uncle. Napoleon began his military training at the age of nine in Briennes, not far from the Ardennes region of France, where Donald's story ends. Covering this circle of life, if you will, traces many of the ups and downs of humanity and leads us to deliberations that cross multiple bridges of time. Surely, like me, and perhaps you, Bonaparte walked in the warm glow of the sunshine on the hillsides of rural France. It can be stunningly beautiful. Nevertheless, our travels, both personally unique, passionate, and emotional, remain incredibly distinct.

A young Wilhelm Gehl also lived in the small community of Schierschwende. Wilhelm, at ten years of age, could better grasp the chaos surrounding his home and the peril his family faced as Napoleon's army marched through their homeland. Mothers and their children never left their properties. The men in this quiet community worked the fields and prayed, knowing the dangers their families faced every day.

Wilhelm was born in 1803, just as Erfurt became part of Prussia, and for the next few decades he witnessed the conflict, destruction, and swings of power between Napoleon and various European allies and coalitions. The conflicts were not trivial. In 1806, during the Battle of Jena, near Erfurt, two hundred thousand troops clashed, leaving behind over thirty thousand casualties. By 1807, the year of Margaretha's birth, the region had been seized by the French polity as part of the defeat of the Fourth Coalition.[1] However, the conflict continued for years to come. In 1807, Napoleon visited the strategic location of Erfurt to inspect the fortifications. He returned in 1813, ordering the citadels to prepare for a siege. By 1813, the conflict reached a pinnacle involving over half a million soldiers.[2] There is little doubt that the young Wilhelm and Margaretha, ten and six years old and living nearby at this time, witnessed multiple tragedies of war. The most significant and bloodiest battle, dubbed The Battle of Nations, took place a short distance away in nearby Leipzig in what was documented as one of the bloodiest battles in the Napoleonic wars. Casualties were high, with over 100,000 dead; thousands of citizens of Erfurt perished in large numbers as refugees fled to Erfurt and surrounding regions. For Wilhelm and Margaretha, death lay at their doorstep from an incredibly early age.

George Robert Gleig,[3] the noted scholar and military writer, wrote in *The Battle of Leipsic*, published in 1852, that "Napoleon held his course from Frankfort by Hanau, Eisenach, and Gotha to Erfurt." By April 1813, twenty-two battalions were posted at Eisenach preparing for the war. Napoleon's army had marched through the local valleys and streams by the homes of Margaretha and Wilhelm. They needed supplies and wreaked havoc in the region.

> *The men, left to forage for themselves, ran hither and thither at will, gathering fuel from whatever quarter promised to afford it with the readiest facility. On such occasions not the gardens and orchards only, but houses themselves suffered. Roofs stripped off, doors torn off, furniture broken up for firewood, these outrages occurred continually.*[4]

The ravages that the army left as they progressed through the region culminated in a series of major battles in Leipsic in the fall of 1813. By that time, Gleig notes there were "heaps of dead and dying in the streets … burned carcasses of men and horses … a lamentable picture of the horrors of war."[5] Despite the ravages of Napoleon, his Prussian campaign was a complete failure, and he was forced to retreat to Paris, where he was later overthrown. By early 1814, the Coalition forces marched into Erfurt, and in a vengeful act, they burned and destroyed Napoleon's ceremonial monument – a symbol of the French oppression.

During this time, Margaretha and Wilhelm were living just outside of Eisenach in Schierschwende. The area was flourishing with farms that were fertile and well cared for by the community. However, as young children, Wilhelm and Margaretha found themselves trapped in a conflict they could not understand. Without question, war imposes many serious repercussions on everyone, leaving behind physical and mental scars that can last a lifetime. There is little doubt these effects weigh most heavily on children. As I contemplate the lives of Donald's ancestors, it is often difficult to put myself in their place, especially in the case of children. In considering their pain and trauma, let us reflect on some of the more recent examples of war-affected children that permeate our daily news. Joanna Barbara states that listing the impacts of war on children is "a sadly straightforward task."[6] She cites death, injury, disability, illness, rape, forced prostitution for subsistence, psychological suffering, moral and spiritual impacts, social and cultural losses, and the recruitment of child soldiers as the types of trauma war-affected children endure.

Children may also lose the love and care of their parents in periods of conflict. Alternative care, orphanages, and refugee camps may provide some relief, but they still inflict a disruption to a child's being that adversely impacts their life and survival, both physically and mentally. We are all too familiar with news, in recent years, of Central American refugees losing their children at the Mexico–American border under the United States' "no tolerance" policies. Such policies separated parents and children, often leading to absurd practices such as toddlers appearing in court. Given a permanent designation of "unaccompanied children," the kids are thrust into care facilities and forced to endure the separation and deportation of their families. The Truth and Reconciliation Commission of Canada also brought attention to inhumane conditions that Indigenous children were forced to live with in residential schools. Some died and were buried in unmarked graves. The young ones who survived carried the resulting trauma a lifetime.

In African Sudan, and various other countries in conflict, militias recruit and force children to fight. Some witness the death of their family members while others are forced to fire the fatal weapons themselves. Children do not escape the brutalities of war and oppression. These memories endure and affect the lives of these children, and their children, for generations.

It is incredible that humankind cannot seem to step beyond the cruelty that is cast upon our young ones. In recent times, hundreds of thousands of children have become casualties of war every year.[7] Every. Damn. Year. Their lives are cut short, they are disabled, or they are crammed into refugee camps without nutrition and clean water, perpetuating an enduring crisis. Children may lose their moral structure and be forcibly recruited into a military force. War-affected children experience depression and anxiety. For girls especially, rape, pregnancy, and exposure to sexually transmitted diseases such as HIV/AIDS devastates their childhood.

The natural curiosity of children often leads them to expose themselves to dangers even after a conflict ends. In 2016 alone, there were more than 1500 child casualties resulting from interactions with landmines, with almost 500 children dead.[8] The survivors, often losing a limb, may be lucky to acquire a prosthetic, but rehabilitation services are usually severely lacking.

All of this occurs within the context of our "modern society." Speaking to the United Nations Security Council in May 2022 concerning the devastating effects of the Russian invasion of Ukraine[9] on their children, UNICEF Deputy Executive Director Omar Abdi reported that:

"in just this past month, the UN verified that nearly one hundred children were killed, and we believe the actual figures to be considerably higher. More children have been injured and have faced grave violations of their rights; millions more have been displaced. Schools continue to be attacked and used for military purposes, and water and sanitation infrastructure has been impacted. The war in Ukraine, like all wars, is a child protection and child rights crisis."

In the Erfurt Province of Wilhelm's and Margaretha's childhood, especially during the Battle of Leipzig near their home, the substantial number of casualties and refugees would no doubt have led to a heartbreaking disruption of their daily existence, including malnutrition and the spread of infectious diseases. The children, as Abdi asserts, would be unduly affected. The general terror and horror of Wilhelm and Margaretha's experiences would understandably lead to anxiety and depression, disruption of their childhood and formative years, and personal loss. Clearly many children carry these scars, with such inflictions impacting their personal existence and relationships. While many of these children wear the wounds on their sleeves; others may remain more subdued as they search for peace, better opportunities, and a peaceful community.

War happens. People's lives can be shattered, houses destroyed, civilizations ruined — but Wilhelm and Margaretha were survivors. Whether merely witnesses or grim victims of the Napoleonic conflicts we do not really know, but they owned the extraordinary will to preserve their legacy. However, at that moment in time, their lives had become tragically engulfed in an historical crisis unfolding on their doorstep.

Life goes on even when you think it cannot, and in the aftermath of the historical conflict and upheaval, Wilhelm and Margaretha married in 1830 and started to raise a family, recovering from the devastation of the Napoleonic wars. But like many inhabitants in the Erfurt province of central Germany, the youthful and industrious Wilhelm Gehl and Margaretha Gross struggled to manage their affairs following the turmoil of the Napoleonic wars. In the subsequent years, political unrest grew locally in the aftermath of these conflicts, amid heavy taxation and censorship, as a new Germany began to materialize. The dawn of the Industrial Revolution led to labour strife, and protests in the streets laid the foundation for German unification, culminating in the revolution of 1848.

By 1844, Wilhelm and his wife Margaretha, with seven children ages three to fourteen, could no longer tolerate the upheaval in their community. So they boarded the ship *Familian*, which set sail for America from the port of Bremen, Germany. The family embarked on a journey to Canada, where, in the years to follow, they would become Donald's grandparents in a land far away.

* * *

Travelling with children in tow is no easy task in the 21st century. We've all been there, remember? We secure the kids in a child or booster seat and manage the feeding frenzy and toilet stops for two, or maybe three children at most. Our tote bags ride in the back of the SUV filled with diapers, wipes, sanitizer, and age-appropriate refreshments. We carry the necessary snacks, Gravol, medicines, and band-aids. Our "devices" are programmed with apps and entertainment to divert attention from the tantrums and sibling rivalry. Everyone has a cell phone, and the most stressful challenge is who gets to decide what DVD to play in the entertainment centre.

Now imagine the challenges of travelling with a family of seven children, in the 1800s, to a new land across the ocean. You must first get to a port of departure, travelling by foot, cart, or maybe river boat if you are lucky. Taking a train was not an option for Wilhelm and Margaretha, who crossed 400 km overland to get from their home near Erfurt to the port of departure in Bremen. The kids, Florence, thirteen; Anton, eleven; Carl, nine; Georg, seven; Catherine, five; Fredericka, three; and Maria, one, were led by their parents on a journey that spanned many days. Once they reached Bremen, emigrants would normally spend some time in the port area before boarding a ship. Those with means could stay in nearby inns, and the less fortunate took sanctuary in large wooden sheds or in barns along the shoreline. Food and shelter would be necessary, and for a large family like the Gehls, costs often escalated in the port area as thousands of other travelers arrived to compete for resources and complete their own voyages. Thieves and scam artists took advantage of the vulnerable migrating masses.

The city of Bremen, established in the 9th century, is situated on the Weser River in northern Germany, near the North Sea. As silt clogged the channel to the sea, the city eventually extended to Bremerhaven on the North Sea and became a major seaport for emigration from Germany to America. Millions of anxious immigrants to America passed through the harbour in the 19th century. Wilhelm and Margaretha Gehl, kids in tow, somehow managed to find their way to Bremen, where they first boarded an overcrowded barge to take them the fifty kilometers from Bremen to the port. Ultimately, they sailed on the "barque" *Familian* to America. The

Familian was a three-masted seafaring vessel with the foremast and mainmast square rigged, and a third mast, the mizzenmast, fore and aft rigged. The barque had no engines; they were solely guided by the energy of the wind.

In the era of the Internet and television, we are all too often reminded of the treachery of boat crossings of immigrants. Recently, over one million migrants have fled Middle Eastern and African countries by boat across the Mediterranean Sea. Fleeing war torn countries like Syria, Iraq, and Libya, most were seeking refugee status in the European Union. The sea crossings were dangerous. Over ten thousand migrants perished in shipwrecks in the period from 2014 – 2017 [10], including infants, whose pictures on daily news reports stunned the world.

At the turn of the 19th century, immigration from Europe to America increased substantially and ocean crossings were even more hazardous than the tragedies we witness today. The vast majority of migrants were crowded into steerage, the area below the main deck where freight was stored. Few laws were in place at this time to oversee conditions passengers experienced on board the migrant ships. Consequently, conditions were uncomfortable in the best scenario, and hazardous in most cases. All vessels at this time were sailing ships, often doubling as cargo vessels. On one voyage they may carry beef and pigs, and on another human travelers. Ventilation below deck was secured through iron hatches, and the toilets – buckets in crowded spaces – were in such dismal shape that the smell was usually intolerable. Complaints were common about food and water, as well as the offensive behaviour of the crew, especially with respect to women traveling alone. [11] In many cases, migrants had to bring their own food; if food was provided it was usually rationed.

The steerage area was generally made of rough sawn timber, and passengers had to supply their own bedding. Disease spread quickly. It was not uncommon for migrant ships to have several hundred passengers in steerage, and ships were often quarantined upon arrival because of ill and dying passengers. Many ports became quarantine centres. In Canada, Grosse Isle Quebec was a common port of entrance that checked arrivals for their health.

A cabin passenger on a barque that arrived at Grosse Isle in 1847 from Ireland describes, in detail, the horror of his voyage and the conditions in general of migrant ships:

> *In only ten of the vessels that arrived at Montreal in July, four from Cork and six from Liverpool, out of 4,427 passengers, 804 had died on the passage, and 847 were sick on their arrival; that is, 847 were visibly diseased, for the result proves that a far larger number had in them the seeds of disease.*[12]

On board this ship food was rationed, with one pound of meal or bread for each adult, half a pound for each individual under fourteen, and one third of a pound for each child under seven. The water was described as "foul, muddy, and bitter from having been in a wine cask," and the men complained of starvation and the lack of water to make drinks for their sick wives and children. On this trip, one man lost his wife, hurriedly buried at sea within an hour of her demise, a baby was born on board, and other deaths were expected.

Vessels at this port arrived daily from a variety of departure ports, including Liverpool, Le Havre, Hamburg, and Bremen. A cabin passenger, writing of his experiences onboard the Irish ship, noted that as his ship lay quarantined in Grosse Isle, two ships from Bremen came in the morning and were discharged at once, having no sickness. He recounted that over five hundred passengers, "all of them (without a single exception) comfortably and neatly clad, clean, and happy."[13] Wilhelm, Margaretha, and their seven children were perhaps fortunate enough to embark on a ship like this, but such a ship was usually an exception rather than the rule.

The ships from Bremen did not always provide the easiest of voyages, but they were more accommodating in their efforts than other ports of departure. By the 1830s the migrant business was booming, and Bremen quickly became the leading port for immigrants to America. The local government, wanting to attract more emigrants, established laws governing the seaworthiness of ships, minimum space needs, and sufficient provisions. They required a doctor and mandatory sanitary inspections for all vessels. Ultimately, Bremen became the leading port for emigration from Europe and thrived additionally by importing American goods back to Germany. It was many years before other ports began to mimic the success of Bremen.

Despite these conditions – at times pitiful, at times barely livable – Wilhelm and Margaretha, and their seven children, arrived in New York city on July 22, 1844. Their arrival was certainly a cause for celebration. One commentator described the resiliency of the migrants he observed:

Yet – untutored, degraded, famished, and plague-stricken, as they were; I assert that there was more true heroism, more faith, more forgiveness to their enemies, and submission to the Divine Will, exemplified in these victims, than could be found in ten times the number of their oppressors.[14]

The characteristics of faith and compassion would certainly apply to Wilhelm and Margaretha and the undertaking they faced with seven young children. Can you imagine their spirit as they stood on solid ground with these children at their side? In a spirit of euphoria, the Irish would break out in a jig to a fiddle tune as they stepped from their ships. The Gehls, elated to have finally left behind the memories and anguish of war, were a bit more reserved in their demeanour. No doubt disembarking from the *Familian* was joyful, but a new, strange world awaited the fatigued family. At this time, there was no immigrant arrival centre [15] in New York. The shipping company submitted a passenger listing to the Customs officer, and each immigrant made the necessary declarations.

The Gehl family passenger log on the Familian

The family could, for a day's rest, stay in a nearby *Gasthof* that commonly catered to German immigrants, but their journey was not complete. From New York, some German immigrants ventured to nearby Pennsylvania (usually the Mennonites). Others followed a route up the Hudson River to the Erie Canal and on to Buffalo. They completed their journey by covered wagon, or by foot, as they crossed the plains to reach their final destination in Waterloo County, Ontario, Canada.

Mennonites, many who migrated from Pennsylvania, had purchased large tracts of land in Waterloo County, Ontario, near the Grand River and the surrounding region as early as the turn of the 19th century. The first German Catholic immigrants settled on land that was adjacent to this Mennonite colony. John James Jones, author of *The Emigrants Guide*, cites the favourable benefits of coming to Canada, where labour was much appreciated and "the results of sobriety, diligence, and hard work invariably flow into his own pockets rather than into those of others."[16] For Jones, strong arms and quick hands, as well as shrewd heads that knew how to use them, were the greatest form of capital. The poorest farmer, with diligence and hard work, could double, triple, or even quadruple their wealth with the most important credentials, according to Jones; moral qualifications.

Wilhelm and Margaretha, devout Catholics survivors with sincere moral convictions, and seven children, quickly settled in and began to farm some land near Heidelberg, Ontario. Not long after their arrival in December 1845, another son, Reinhardt, was born. In the following years, three more children followed. The Gehls became a family of two parents and eleven children. Sadly, Wilhelm passed away in 1856 at the age of fifty-three. The challenges of his life included enduring an historic conflict and a journey halfway around the world with a young family. The hard work of a settler farmer clearing and breaking the land took its toll. Wilhelm, with his gritty efforts, had built a modest farm and left in his will one hundred and sixty-six acres and "all the stock and farming utensils and house furniture"[17] to be divided evenly between the children as his "beloved" Margaretha determined it was appropriate. Margaretha, forty-nine years of age and mother of eleven children, assumed the role of the head of the household. Life was hard for immigrant women, and Margaretha herself passed away at the age of fifty-eight. Reinhardt was eleven years old when his father Wilhelm died, the same age as his father when he was witnessing the devastation of the Napoleonic conflicts. The young Reinhardt, in the footsteps of his dad, persevered, first in farming and then becoming a farrier, and finally a veterinary surgeon in nearby Heidelberg. At twenty-three years of age, Reinhardt married Mary Ann Woods. Mary Ann, just sixteen years old, was born in Waterloo County in 1853. Her mother, Sally Ann Woods, had immigrated to the region from Edgefield in Norfolk County, England and at nineteen years of age gave birth as a single mother to Mary Ann. Such was the life of the local immigrant families; teenage motherhood was not unusual at this time and women often had ten or more children. Reinhardt and Mary Ann were no exception, raising eleven children of their own. One of the children, Rosetta Gehl, was born June 29, 1890, in Heidelberg. Rosetta would become Donald's mother.

Donald had never met his great grandparents, Wilhelm and Margaretha, but their legacy and innumerable life's challenges were instrumental in establishing his family history. There is no question that Wilhelm and Margaretha possessed a work ethic that demanded endurance in the face of austerity, agony, and conflict. Wilhelm guided his family from a small village in Germany in the midst of a destructive war – an historic conflict – to set up a small farm in southern Ontario. He provided his family with the means for their future survival. Margaretha bore eleven children; she fed them, cared for them, and carried them halfway around the world. She became a widow much too early, with several of her children still under the age of ten years. Her stamina and courage are unfathomable, and she was a striking example of the hard work and unrecognized contributions that immigrant women always made for their spouses, children, and countries. For Donald, his maternal ancestry passed on a resilient work ethic and determination to survive in the most demanding circumstances. As difficult as it may seem, Donald's paternal ancestry, also German immigrants, emerged from a different yet equally heartless and impoverished setting.

Footnotes Chapter 2

[1] The Wars of the Coalitions (1st – 7th) began in the later part of the 18th century and continued until Napoleon's defeat and permanent exile in 1815. The Fourth Coalition (1806–1807) consisted of the countries of Prussia, Russia, Saxony, Sweden and Britain.

[2] By this time the Sixth Coalition.

[3] G. R. Gleig, *The Leipsic Campaign*, (Longman, Brown, Green and Longmans, London: 1852). Gleig was also a member of Wellington's army, which marched into France in 1814 for Napoleon's abdication.

[4] Gleig, "Leipsic," 26.

[5] Gleig, "Leipsic," 248.

[6] Joanna Santa Barbara, "Impact of War on Children and Imperative to End War," *Croation Medical Journal 47*, no. 6 (December 2006): 891–894.

[7] G. Machel, "The impact of armed conflict on children: report of the expert of the secretary general of the United Nations." New York: United Nations; 1996: http://www.unicef.org/graca/a51-306_en.pdf.

[8] "2017 Landmine Monitor, International Campaign to Ban Landmines – Cluster Munition Coalition (ICBL-CMC)": http://www.the-monitor.org/en-gb/reports/2017/landmine-monitor-2017.aspx.

[9] UNICEF press release, May 12, 2022, https://www.unicef.org/press-releases/children-ukraine-need-end-war-their-futures-hang-balance.

Footnotes cont'd

[10] International Organization for Migration, "Migrant Fatalities 2014 – 2017", https://missingmigrants.iom.int.

[11] The distinguished historian Josef Polišenský notes that as far as it is known, no one was ever prosecuted for these crimes.

[12] By A Cabin Passenger, *Voyage To Quebec In An Irish Emigrant Vessel. Embracing Quarantine At Grosse Isle In 1847. With Notes Illustrative Of The Ship-Pestilence Of That Fatal Year..* (Coolidge And Wiley, 1848): 12.

[13] *Voyage To Quebec*, 91.

[14] *Voyage To Quebec*, 18.

[15] Castle Gardens opened in 1855, while the most often cited immigrant processing centre, Ellis Island, was not in place until 1890.

[16] John Jones, *The Emigrants Guide*, (International Employment & Emigration Agency, London: 1885): 5.

[17] Probate of the Will of Wilhelm Gehl, late of the Township of Waterloo, granted the 2nd day of July 1856. Petition of Anton Gehl and Margaret Gehl. Surrogate Court Records Copybook Register A 1853-1871 transcript to 1863. Frances Hoffman transcriber.

Chapter 3

No Place For Us

Go then, there are other worlds than these.

– Stephen King

Seventeen-year-old Sophia's face was strained, her eyes swelled with tears. Her older husband-to-be announced they would be leaving Mecklenburg, Germany, for North America. The voyage would be long and difficult, but a colony in Canada would welcome them; they could build a new life and raise a family. The year was 1856. At this time, and in this culture, young women typically lived under the control of their father; in marriage, their duty was handed to their husbands. Sophia was a typical young woman. She was destined to be a wife and mother in support of her spouse and family to make ends meet. She had little choice but to follow the path of her husband on a long and arduous journey in life.

G. W. Warr[1] described three different classes of migrants during this period. There was the poor man struggling in vain against adversity in his homeland. He was joined by a stream of emigrants crawling to a strange land where they'd been told poverty did not exist. The second kind was the man of means who embarked with eagerness, hearing of wealth amassed with rapidity and ease. Finally, there was the youthful and talented individual who followed the fortunes of their profession, where less competition and greater rewards abounded. There was little doubt that Sophia's husband-to-be, Henry, was the poor man living in destitute conditions.

Donald's grandfather Henry Metz was born in Hessen, Germany in 1820 to a underprivileged Mennonite family. Henry later relocated to Mecklenburg as a farm labourer, where he met his future wife, the young Sophia Schultz. As a peasant labourer, the thirty-eight-year-old Henry had limited opportunities to establish and support a family. His only choice was to follow the thousands of other people from Mecklenburg fleeing their homeland, often with the support of the local government.

Mecklenburg is a region in northeast Germany near the Baltic Sea, east of Hamburg. The land is fertile, with rolling hills and gentle rivers flowing across the state. Fritz Reuter, a popular German author, lived and wrote extensively about life in the area during the 19th century. Born and raised in Mecklenburg to an established family, Reuter recognized the political instability of the district and the deplorable conditions of the peasantry. He wrote broadly about the plight of the common people, and his works were widely recognized by the 1850s in the country and beyond. Reuter's thoughts on the Mecklenburg ladies from this era seem most fitting for Sophia:

> *The wife came. She was a young, pretty woman; it was not long since she had been running about, a young girl, as fresh and bright as only our Mecklenburg country girls can be, but now sickness had washed off the maiden roses from her cheeks, and household labor had made the soft, rounded outlines a little angular – our housewives in the country grow old early.*[2]

Reuter's prose fittingly described the seventeen-year-old Sophia living in desperate circumstances with limited freedom. In Mecklenburg, childhood was "little more than the physical inability to participate fully in agricultural labour."[3] For young girls, starting around seven years of age, childhood meant looking after younger children, picking berries and herbs for tea, and gathering firewood. Adolescent girls became maids and were subjected to long hours and exhausting regimes that included milking cows, feeding pigs, cleaning manure from the pens, spinning wool, and performing a wide array of household chores. Many of the nobility considered maids to be their "property" and "sexual assaults on young maids by both nobles and administrators were not uncommon."[4] For the peasant class, emigration would be a new chance in life, an opportunity to raise your family in a new, more prosperous, and peaceful environment. For the youthful Sophia, the chaos wrought by the aftermath of the Napoleonic wars – the merging of city-states, kingdoms, and principalities, combined with poverty and feudalism – pressed her to stand tall, to persevere and pursue a new life in a new land.

Napoleon had been defeated at Waterloo in 1815, but his wars had lasting effects on the state of Europe. In the ensuing years, Mecklenburg struggled through a period of serious economic depression. Ultimately, the chaos of war, political upheaval, and an impending industrial revolution disrupted the social fabric, impacting the German peasantry in the most discriminatory ways. In the early nineteenth century, feudalism was how the nobility managed the peasanty; serfdom was the mode of living for peasants. Serfs were mandated to work on the land of their owner. They cultivated the land, worked to recover the resources in the mines, and maintained the general infrastructure of the countryside. In return, they were granted a small plot of land to support their own sustenance.

In 1820, the year of Henry's birth, serfdom was abolished in Mecklenburg. This apparent progress in the social structure was met with resistance from landowners who did not want to pay their workers. Such recalcitrance initially led landowners to manage their farms with a minimum of labourers, making it difficult for the peasant workers in Mecklenburg to find a means to support themselves. An individual born in Mecklenburg at this time belonged to the city or village where they were born, or the community where they could receive the rights of establishment.[5] All labourers like Henry, who were born outside of the region, were paid a pittance for their work and were refused the right of establishment by the ruling class.

It was not unusual for a farm labourer to enter into a relationship with a young peasant maid. However, they needed permission to marry before they could begin a family, and the granting of the right to marry was subject to the granting of the right of establishment. As a result, a man or woman who did not have the right of establishment could never marry and establish a home. Moreover, the residents who worked as poorly paid labourers were only given a limited right to residence, and only for as long as they had work. Social conditions had deteriorated, and Mecklenburgers like Henry and Sophia effectively became displaced in their own country. Fritz Reuter wrote several works that reflected life in Mecklenburg at the time:

> *Mecklenburg is a beautiful and a rich land, just the kind of country that delights a farmer, but at the time of which I am speaking there was great poverty and distress throughout the length and breadth of it, and the collector knocked at every door,*

and demanded that the rent should be paid, and whoever had anything to give, gave his last penny, and he who had nothing to give was sold up.[6]

Sold up! In other words, they were evicted. Fritz Reuter also reflected these sentiments eloquently in his poetry. In one poem, he wrote, *"Kein Platz für uns"* – there is no place for us, nobody wants to welcome us. Henry and Sophia were not alone; along with thousands of other peasant labourers, they found no place for themselves in their homeland. Ironically, as the aristocracy marginalized the peasantry, the lack of farm labourers led to a general degradation of the community. The landowners hired fewer workers, and local conditions declined. Reuters reported that:

The farm-buildings had never been very substantial, and were now much in need of repair, and moreover, things were very disorderly.[7]

The infrastructure crumbled, and people often experienced daily challenges like those faced today in neglected and impoverished regions of our own lands. Even today, we find poor conditions within many of our communities, such as poorly supported neighbourhoods, homeless camps, accumulation of refuse, and roads full of potholes. Potholes are ubiquitous, and in the face of such wearisome conditions, Mecklenburgers never seemed to lose their sense of humour. As Reuter described:

… an old peasant was standing by his hedge, throwing stones, as big and round as the brim of your hat, into the holes in the road. In some places in Mecklenburg this is what they call "mending the roads". [8]

Reuter also described the harshness of life, as the ruling class commonly beat their workers. One episode involved the story of a homeowner who, unhappy with the maid servant, beat her severely with fire-tongs. The village doctor treated the victim and reported the woman to the authorities. Although the homeowner was admonished for such cruelty[9], it was noted that "if she had made use of a pudding-stick, of the same length and thickness, they would have done nothing to her."[10] This is reminiscent of our own familiar phrase, "the rule of thumb", long thought to have been advanced by an Irish magistrate in the 17th century as the defining width of a switch that a husband could use to beat his wife.

By the 1840s, unrest spread in the streets as more peasants became destitute and homeless. In 1847, a famine spread in the region, and Fritz Reuter reported that:

The scarcity was universal, and it had come over the blessed land like a thief in the night, so no one had thought of it, no one had prepared for it.[11]

Few options remained for residents like Henry and Sophia, wedged in the lower social class. They were not alone – between 1820 and 1890, over 250,000 Mecklenburgers left their home, driven by social unrest in the transition from the feudal structure to the capitalist system. Between 1851 and 1860 alone, over 50,000 Mecklenburgers, including Henry and Sophia in 1856, emigrated overseas, mostly to the United States but also to South America and Canada, usually through the port at Hamburg. Young maids like Sophia were not considered legal persons, and they needed their parents' permission to emigrate. Emigration and boarding fees amounted to about three years of farm labour, and many couples, like Henry and Sophia, travelled to Hamburg by train, then married on board the ship or at the port of departure.

Steamships were rare and expensive to board, so as many as ninety-five percent of emigrants had to cross the ocean on a three-masted vessel under dreadful conditions. Joanne Flint describes the ocean crossing from Hamburg of a young Greta Janzen in 1874:

> *For twenty terrible days Greta and her family lived at sea. At night they slept below deck on mattresses that shifted when the small ship rolled and pitched ... The passengers were fed only flour soup and bread and butter. This combined with the continual rocking motion of the boat, made Greta sick to her stomach. Two weeks into the voyage, she watched sadly as the bodies of two young children, wrapped in rough canvas and weighted down with iron bars, were buried at sea.[12]*

Henry and his young wife Sophia faced similar challenges as they set sail for a new land. Most emigrants from Mecklenburg arrived in North America via New York. From there they often travelled by train or ship to rural Midwestern states such as Iowa and Michigan. Some headed for the urban centres of Milwaukee or Chicago[13], whose industrial expansions attracted craftsmen and skilled labour. Others, often the poor labourers and maids like Henry and Sophia, migrated to Pennsylvania or Upper Canada.

Mennonites had started to arrive in Upper Canada around the time of the American revolution in 1776. Some came directly to Canada, but most of them found their way through Pennsylvania which had a sustained tradition, starting in the seventeenth century, of Mennonite immigration. Leaving behind the hardships and prejudices of Mecklenburg, they stepped into a world of opportunity that remained centred on hard work and resiliency. Life was not easy, and women – especially young women – faced a lifetime tasked with enormous workloads. In *Mennonite Women in Canada*, Marlene Epp writes about the trials of Barbara Schultz, who, similar to Sophia, was only sixteen when she married her twenty-eight-year-old husband and immigrated to Canada in 1824. Arriving in New York and then proceeding on to Pennsylvania, they acquired oxen and a wagon to make the trek to Waterloo township for settlement. Barbara, a young mother like Sophia, bore eighteen children and faced a difficult life. Epp describes Barbara's life as:

> … *characterized by the demanding and constant physical labour of subsistence production and the equally constant bodily changes she experienced from continuous reproduction.*[14]

Shortly before her last child's first birthday, Barbara's husband passed away. Still she persisted, working from early morning to late in the evening to keep her children warm, fed, clothed, and sheltered. Caring for children was not the only task Mennonite women faced. They planted and harvested huge gardens, cut and preserved meat, made soap and candles, and wove and sewed clothes. Barbara Schultz lived for thirty years past her husband's death, endangering her own health to lay the groundwork for her children's future. Sophia's life followed a similar path. The women, from their teens to old age, faced a daily routine of demanding work; following the death of their older spouses, they raised the children alone. Moreover, as if these burdens and harsh challenges were insufficient, the women also faced sexist tirades. In one case, a reprehensible male decried that "Many women are like coins. Worth only their face value." Was his blatant disrespect to women whispered on the side to his macho companions? No, it was published in the local paper[15] along with other "manly" invectives on a regular basis.

> Many women are like coins. Worth only their face value.
>
> The only housework that some girls do is when they begin to dust after a beau.

Berlin Daily News November 29, 1879; Source: Kitchener Public Library Archives

Sophia had emigrated to the Waterloo County region, where her husband, Henry, had joined a Mennonite community as a farm labourer. From 1825 to 1870, many Mennonites settled on crown land near New Hamburg, Ontario, where the community still exists today. They brought with them their German heritage and language, their religion and communal way of living, and their observance of pacifism. Henry and Sophia stayed on the farm their whole lives, where they raised eleven children. The last of the children, Aaron, was born in 1881 when his father Henry was sixty-one years old. Henry passed away in 1893 when Aaron was just twelve years old. The family was reflective of a large segment of German immigrants in the Waterloo County region. They were strongly religious Mennonites, pacifists in nature, and often penniless farmers.

At the turn of the century, life on the farm did not suit Aaron very well, and in the nearby village of Heidelberg, the young Rosetta Gehl attracted his attention. Aaron was ten years her senior, but they had much in common. Their parents were both immigrants from Germany, fleeing a society demoralized by Napoleon's wars and the transition from serfdom and dynastic rule to a capitalistic society. Aaron's older brother, George, and Rosetta's father, Reinhard, were both farriers and they certainly knew each other well. In a growing rural area, shoeing horses and tending animals was an engaging business. In a small community it was not hard to know who was your competition.

Although Aaron and Rosetta both recently came from large immigrant families and German backgrounds, in terms of religion, they were very incompatible. Aaron, twenty-nine years old at this time, came from a conservative Mennonite family, and Rosetta, still a teenager of nineteen years, came from a staunchly Catholic household. Maybe they saw themselves as Romeo and Juliet; but the families were certainly the Montagues and Capulets.

Aaron stayed with his family on the colony farm until after his mother, Sophia, died on January 11, 1909. In the following year, buoyed by his newly discovered freedom, Aaron courted Rosetta, and they quickly wed a short time later on May 3, 1910. Two of Aaron's brothers had already left the colony farm; Henry Jr. migrated to Kansas and William to Manitoba. Aaron, the youngest in a family of eleven children, was ready to follow in their footsteps. But Rosetta, still close to her family and her father, insisted their children be raised Catholics. Aaron agreed, and he left the farm and his family behind while promising to raise their children in the Catholic tradition. A clash of religions never seems to result in a peaceful settlement. As a result, after they married, little contact was maintained between Aaron and the rest of his family.[16]

Both of the Gehl and Metz families had fled Germany. Their journeys were long and arduous, especially for the women. Both women, Margaretha and Sophia, gave birth to eleven children while they managed their households, mirroring their strong work ethic and profound religious principles. This heritage was a hallmark for their families on the rugged road to happiness and prosperity. Yet as they modelled the role of women in these times, the paternal attitudes towards women in society would be hard to shed. For the men in the family, it was years to come.

Two couples, Henry and Sophia Metz, and Wilhelm and Margaretha Gehl, were driven from their German homeland by war and poverty. They had little to say about any of their living conditions; the only option available to them, and thousands of others like them, was emigration. They passionately embraced this opportunity to begin a new life in a new land, where the only obstacle to a decent standard of living for their families was hard work. Consequently, a strong work ethic was passed on to their children when Aaron and Rosetta began their family in the nearby town of Berlin, Ontario. The immigrants, or so it seemed, could leave the atrocities of war behind as they built a prosperous future for their children at the turn of the 20th century.

Footnotes Chapter 3

[1] G. W. Warr, *Canada As It Is: The Emigrant's Friend And Guide To Upper Canada*, (London: William Edward Painter, Strand. 1847).

[2] Fritz Reuter, *Seedtime and Harvest*, Project Gutenberg: 818.

Footnotes cont'd

[3] Monica Blaschke, "No Way But Out: German Women in Mecklenburg" in *Peasant Maids, City Women, From The European Countryside To Urban America*, edited by Christiane Harzig, (Cornell University Press, Ithaca and London, 1997): 33.

[4] Blaschke, "No Way", 39.

[5] For a detailed historical discussion see Ernst Boll, Abriss der Mecklenburgischen Landeskunde, Naturkunde, Geschichte und Topographie, (Hinstorff'sche Hofbuchhandlung, 1861).

[6] Excerpt From: Fritz Reuter, *An Old Story of My Farming Days (1862)*, (Ut Mine Stromtid), iBooks:18

[7] Excerpt From: Fritz Reuter, *Seed-time and Harvest*, iBooks: 35.

[8] Excerpt From: Fritz Reuter, *In the Year '13: A Tale of Mecklenburg Life (1867)*, iBooks: 306.

[9] Excerpt From: Fritz Reuter. *An Old Story of My Farming Days*, (Ut Mine Stromtid). iBooks. P.37. Translator's note: "the feudal-system was kept up longer in Mecklenburg than elsewhere – the peasantry belonged to the estate and always continued to work on it. A Mecklenburg squire often beat his labourers when he was angry with them."

[10] Excerpt From: Fritz Reuter. *Seed-time and Harvest*, iBooks.1586.

[11] Reuter, *Seed-time*, 200.

[12] Joanne Flint, *The Mennonite Canadians*, (Nelson Canada, 1983):37.

[13] Christiane Harzig, "Creating a Community, German-American Women in Chicago," in *Peasant Maids, City Women, From The European Countryside To Urban America*, 185.

[14] Marlene Epp, *Mennonite Women in Canada: A History*, (University of Manitoba Press, 2008): 23.

[15] *Berlin Daily News*, November 29, 1879.

Footnotes cont'd

[16] Growing up, I knew no relatives on my grandfather's side of the family. In a strange twist of fate, I later lived down the street in Winnipeg, MB, from the granddaughter of Aaron's brother William, Barbara. We got along very well.

Chapter 4

A New Age

There are far better things ahead than any we leave behind.

– C.S. Lewis[1]

In the early twentieth century, Ontario's government passed legislation to enable the transmission of electric power to various municipalities in the province. Berlin, Ontario, viewed as an industrious community that would be able to benefit from this advancement, was chosen as the location for the "flipping of the switch" of Ontario's new hydro-electric power distribution system. It was October of 1910, and newlyweds Rosetta and Aaron Metz left the farm and rural life behind to step into a new age. Ontario's electric grid network brought about dramatic changes never seen before in the history of humankind.

At this time, the town of Berlin was a busy and blossoming manufacturing center. Several factories producing furniture, shoes, buttons, and clothing could be found. Additionally, There was no single dominant trade, leading to a stable, prosperous, and growing community. Commerce ventures, such as banks and insurance companies, demonstrated the broad approach to economic achievement that was attributed to German industry, perseverance, and practicality. Both of Aaron's and Rosetta's immigrant parents exemplified these qualities in their lives, promoting a strong work ethic in the family.

By 1912, as Berlin approached cityhood, it was said that people throughout Canada talked "with amazement" about Berlin. Across the major cities of the west, Berlin had everywhere a reputation as one of the busiest and most prosperous manufacturing cities of the east.[2]

The emergence of wealthy elites is very common in any era of prosperity, and Berlin was no exception. Prominent families such as the Ebys, Briethaupts, Langs, and Kaufmans took their place in the social order. However, community pride overrode personal economic status as the development of clean water systems, sewage disposal, electricity, and modern public transit targeted a more egalitarian way of life. A better quality of life for all members of the community, despite their status, was valued alongside individual gain. In other words, Berlin, Ontario, in the early parts of the twentieth century, was an ideal place to live and raise a family.

Aaron and Rosetta, now Mr. and Mrs. Metz, moved to nearby Berlin on Foreman Street, and soon after they purchased a house on 197 Benton Street. Aaron became a milkman working for Silverwood's Dairy, and Rosetta managed the family home, raising their children and keeping boarders to help make ends meet. Rosetta's sister, Johanna, who was eighteen years old, lived with them while she worked as a tucker sixty hours a week, earning $300 a year. Reinhardt, Rosetta's father, who passed away in 1929, spent his final months with the family. Whether it was family, or another boarder such as a local police constable, Rosetta cooked, cleaned, and maintained their humble abode.

In early 1912, Aaron and Rosetta welcomed their first-born son, Floyd, into the world. As the couple began their new life with a young family, they were soon confronted with the onset of the First World War. Although fought on a different continent, its effects permeated across the Canadian landscape. It is difficult for most of us today to imagine the pain and anguish that lay at their doorsteps in time of war. In my lifetime, the most recent conflict involving Canada, the Afghanistan war, claimed one hundred and fifty-nine Canadian lives. While the families of the fallen, and close friends, carried and still carry the memory of that loss, most of us know little more than what we read in the news reports years ago. We cannot imagine the burden they continue to bear.

For Aaron and Rosetta, and many of their friends and neighbours, the anguish was widespread. In the First World War, a devastating toll of over 60,000 Canadians perished, leaving very few families untouched by the conflict. If you didn't lose a close family member, your neighbour did. For many families, the loss was not singular. Moreover, it was predominantly young men who were dying and never coming home again.

At the beginning of the war, the German population in the region surrounding Berlin found themselves in a precarious position; their country of origin declared war on their current homeland. Even though many, like the Metz's, were second generation Canadians, the fact that they carried a German name and still spoke the German language left a target on their backs.

All wars bring about internal conflicts. Canadians on the home front coped with disputes such as racial tensions based on ethnicity, and the enforcement of conscription. These issues led to a further divide between English and German, or English and French Canadians. In Berlin, Ontario, and the neighbouring Waterloo County, racial discrimination percolated throughout the community as, in all wars, the "other side" is demonized. Toronto's newspapers were particularly harsh; Globe editors warned that Berliners must be kept "under close observation [as] their presence may be a source of great danger." [3] Many newspaper reports on World War I typically accentuated German atrocities. They reported on the use of poisonous gases, the German mistreatment of prisoners of war, and the cold-blooded murder, with bayonets, of Canadian soldiers. All these reports, sometimes true reflections of the war, were then generalized to the local German population with rhetoric such as "A German's word simply cannot be trusted," and the insinuation of cruelty of "people" who advocated the use of a poisonous gas.[4]

The threats would always be carried to extremes by military recruiters – unhappy with the lack of young men signing up to serve. The district expeditionary forces often took to the streets where they "bullied and bloodied local residents" … while "store windows displaying German goods were smashed, and businesses and clubs looted." [5] The slurs extended to the extremes, as exemplified by Lieutenant Stanley Nelson's [6] threat to the livelihood of Berliners.

The showing that the physically fit young men of North Waterloo have made is so rotten that I have heard an outside businessman say to a traveler from a Berlin wholesale house, 'I'll not buy another damned article manufactured in that German town."

Anyone who dared question the intimidation was also treated harshly. A Lutheran minister, C.R. Tappert, who questioned the truthfulness of some anti-German propaganda, was forcefully removed from his home and beaten "senseless."

Another target of the anti-German hatred at this time was exemplified in the destruction of the statue of Kaiser Wilhelm, erected in Victoria Park only a few minutes from the Metz home on Benton Street. Kaiser Wilhelm (King William IV) led Prussia in victory over France in 1871, establishing Germany as a united nation. Even Fritz Reuter, the Mecklenburg radical, celebrated the birth of the new nation led by the heroic Kaiser. Upon his death in 1888, Wilhelm was honoured in his homeland, and internationally, with the erection of hundreds of monuments as a testament to German pride and nationalism. In Berlin, Ontario, a fourteen-foot memorial statue made in Germany was erected in the summer of 1897 at a well-attended public event.

Statues are typically constructed in the rabid moments of nationalism and patriotism. And then, for years they rest idly until the roots of that patriotism surfaces once more. In America today, this is reflected in the controversies over confederate monuments and the riots in the wake of the George Floyd murder by police in Minneapolis in 2020. It is quite ironic that we erect these statues in a sense of nationalistic patriotism and then ignore them for years as nothing more than a landmark. We grow used to the spaces that the statues occupy and rarely contemplate the person or the cause. How often have you planned to meet someone at an historical monument without reflecting on the meaning of the landmark? The Kaiser's bust was no different, and as the First World War in 1914 started to escalate, British nationalism was on the rise.

German symbols, such as the bust of Kaiser Wilhelm displayed in Victoria Park, were vandalized repeatedly.

The First World War generated discord among the citizens of Waterloo County as the populace was divided by their heritages; German and British. An opinion in the weekly paper underlined the anxiety towards foreigners: "the alien is welcome if he will remember that the native born have certain seniority rights." *Seniority rights,* certainly a term we can relate to in today's world. The expression references a two tier status of citizenship. It reminds me of former Canadian Prime Minister Stephen Harper's reference to "old stock" Canadians.[7] Moreover, the Trump era in the United States clearly articulated the notion of seniority rights of white Americans. In one of his rallies in 2019, Trump's followers chanted "send them back" as Trump critiqued a "squad" of Democratic congresswomen for opposing him. Although, the women of colour were naturalized Americans, they were treated as though they were foreign terrorists. The rhetoric was astounding and uncomfortable for many.

In the first week of the war in 1914, the Kaiser statue was forcibly removed from its pedestal and tossed in the lake at Victoria Park. The bust was subsequently retrieved from the lake and later stored inside the Concordia Club for safe keeping. Like many other ethnic organizations, the Concordia Club was committed to the preservation of the German language, customs, and family traditions. The club organized popular Sangerfests (choir festivals) and other cultural activities, and was a prime meeting place for persons of German origins.

The celebration of German culture did not rest well, among many of the populace, with the advent of the war. By 1916, the Concordia Club was ransacked by members of the 118th Battalion, and once again the Kaiser's bust was removed, mocked publicly, used for target practice, and vandalized repeatedly.[8]

It is not that difficult today to relate to the tensions between opposing world views manifested by the destruction of statues. As I write this paragraph, I am astonished to watch an eerily similar destruction of a statue in the British city of Bristol on local television. In the wake of numerous worldwide demonstrations over the George Floyd fatality[9], anti-racism protestors in Bristol toppled the statue of Edward Colston, a 17th century slave trader. They dragged the statue through the streets and dumped it into the river Avon. The removals of Confederate statues in the United States, such as the General Robert E. Lee statue in Richmond, Virginia; the Imperialist Cecil Rhodes statue in Cape Town, South Africa; and the Sir John A. MacDonald statues in Victoria, B.C. (for his role in the treatment of Native Canadians in residential schools), are but a few examples of Stiem's assertion that statues "embody tension between two world views."[10]

Aaron and Rosetta, living just a few short blocks from the Kaiser's statue, carried a German name and spoke the language fluently. Donald's mother, Rosetta, lived nearby as the Kaiser statue was repeatedly sacked close to home. We often say that history repeats herself, yet rarely think of the often obscure reruns that usually accompany major events. Years earlier, Rosetta's grandmother, Margaretha, resided near the town of Eisenach in Germany where the Napoleon monument was torn down. Both women lived through the repercussions of war, the animosity that it wrought, and they endured. Rosetta, like most of the German residents in the area, was guided by her family's loyalty to their country – Canada. However, in spite of their loyalty to Canadian soil, the nationalistic tensions remained for the family to bear.

A New Age 51

It is a known certainty of war that the "other" side will be demonized, and anyone remotely associated with the other side will be in peril. For example, in 1916, a pavilion at Victoria Park where children commonly played burned to the ground. Rych Miller[11] reports that footprints in the snow suggested an arsonist had set fire to gasoline inside the pavilion's restaurant. The local press suggested that it was an "anti-German" act by an arsonist opposed to the German-born park superintendent. They also speculated that it could have been an "anti-British" act by someone fed up with the antics of the 118th Battalion, who used the hall for drill practice. The 118th Battalion, with its aggressive nature, was often at the forefront of the intercultural battles exasperated by the war.

The Canadian Expeditionary Force (CEF) was the combat troop formation that was designated for service overseas. The CEF consisted of 260 Canadian battalions, and the soldiers were mostly volunteers, stepping forward to serve a patriotic duty to their homeland, Great Britain. However, in various regions of Canada – notably Quebec – recruitment was challenging. In the Waterloo region, the 118th Battalion also had trouble enlisting young men for the war effort. In laying blame, many individuals pointed to German residents, accusing them of sympathizing with Great Britain's enemy. Even the battalion's commanding officer, Lt. Col Lochead, wrote that he struggled with recruiting volunteers from the region because of the "general disloyalty of the community."[12]

The 118th Battalion would march in the streets and use force and coercion to enlist new members. To bolster the regiment's ranks, men were also recruited from outside communities, such as Toronto, bringing with them an additional lack of awareness or understanding of the home-grown German culture and heritage. The 118th Battalion reflected and promoted this rising wave of anti-German sentiment, which cast a forbidding shadow in the region. Indeed, immigrants of German origin were derided and threatened with possible internment. However, given that many of the people of German heritage in the region had actually fled Germany, it was more likely the pacifist nature of the Mennonites which discouraged enrolment.

The anti-German sentiment extended to the name of the city of Berlin itself. A debate emerged in 1916 from the Board of Trade, encouraged by the 118th Battalion and their supporters, to choose a new name for the city. A referendum was declared, a committee was struck, and a list of proposed names for the city was compiled. However, collecting suggestions from the citizenry for names is not always the greatest idea. Do you remember our recent online experiences with Boaty Mcboatface?[13] Many of the submitted suggestions for a new city title included a list of expected patriotic suggestions such as Edwardstown, and Adanac (Canada spelled backwards). Other terms, such as Industria, intended to highlight the city's economy and the amusing Windigo (a mythical cannibalistic monster) were suggested. And, of course, the customary ten-year-old's witticism, Uranus, also made an appearance. Initially, a brief docket of five names; Adanac, Benton, Brock, Corona and Keowana were selected. Then, at the last minute, after his unexpected death on June 5, 1916, the name Kitchener was added to the list. The Secretary of State for War, Lord Kitchener was known for his iconic image on the wartime recruitment posters proclaiming "Your Country Needs You." The vote, held only a few weeks later on the 28th of June, favoured the name Kitchener, and the name of the city changed officially on September 1, 1917. Ten thousand voters were eligible to vote, but only eight hundred and ninety-two showed up at the polls. Three hundred and forty-six votes were cast for the name Kitchener, with a narrow victory margin of just eleven votes.

Obviously, many Germans stayed home on voting day, not willing to change the name of Berlin. However, little was done in terms of protest, as the community, perhaps intimidated by CEF forces, gave up any desire to maintain the status quo. William J. Campbell[14] suggested that the German community's response to the advent of war "mirrored that of many towns," giving support to Britain's interventions. However, he goes on to argue that this "patriotic" response was more of "a community struggling to avoid persecution as it does a population clamouring to make sacrifices in the name of King, Country, and Empire."[15] Campbell writes that Berliners were pragmatic in their approach to the war. They were not "duped by propaganda," they did not volunteer "in droves," nor did they take to protest in the name of ethnic pride.

The youthful Aaron and Rosetta seemed to exemplify Campbell's pragmatic characterization. They only lived a few blocks from Victoria Park and it was a popular spot for the boys and their friends, in the summer for excursions and in winter for ice skating. As the 118th battalion marched through the area, the Metz family minded their own business and stayed at home. However, there is little to suggest that Aaron and Rosetta experienced any harassment. Rosetta's mother, Sarah Jane Woods, was an immigrant from England, and the family likely kept a middle road. The Gehls were also Catholic and fled Germany in 1844, so they were surely familiar with and opposed to the anti-Catholic rhetoric and policies of Kaiser Wilhelm's powerful chancellor, Otto Von Bismarck.

The tragedy of war also hit close to home. Rosetta's younger brother, John Gehl, enlisted for the war effort in 1914.

Interestingly, he did not volunteer for the 118th Battalion, likely because of their anti-German pomposity, but travelled to London, Ontario, to enlist with the 18th Battalion. Two years later, John was killed in action and he lies buried in West-Vlaanderen, Belgium. The assimilation of the family was now complete with their willingness to fight for a united Canada. Following the war, Canada emerged with a new national identity through a recognition of courageous struggles in battles like Vimy Ridge and Passchendaele. The war extracted a heavy toll on the country, as more than 60,000 military personnel were killed. The hardships were compounded when, just as the war was ending, a worldwide outbreak of the Spanish influenza killed another 55,000 Canadians, mostly between twenty and forty years of age.

The 1918 pandemic occurred in a series of three waves in a period of about two years, just as the war was ending. The parallels to the recent Covid-19 outbreak are uncanny. Denial, confusion, racism, resistance, shaming, misinformation, and ignorance were common responses to both crises.

In the summer of 1918, the war dominated the news, with the Allies experiencing success in the trenches while engaging in armistice negotiations. Pockets of enemy resistance still existed and the local news reported on various atrocities. But they also reported over a hundred thousand cases of a virus found in Germany. By July 9, 1918, the *Kitchener News Record* wrote that problems were developing with the German troops, due to the "flanders fever" or "whatever the strange malade may be called."[16] By August, more cases were recounted in the military overseas, and on September 17, the *News Record* described influenza at a military camp in Boston.

At its regular monthly meeting on September 28, the Board of Health reported two cases of measles and none of any other communicable diseases. In response to apprehension that maybe the Spanish influenza had arrived in the city, the Board stated, "enquiry revealed this is not the case."[17] The situation was eerily similar to the onset of the Covid pandemic in our time. In early February 2020, while the virus ravaged Italy and Spain, the United States President Donald Trump[18] claimed that the fifteen cases reported in the US would soon be zero. By mid-February over fifty cases had been reported, and Trump told reporters "We have it very much under control in this country." As cases continued to spiral, he added, "It's going to disappear. One day – it's like a miracle – it will disappear." In mid-March he said, "And it will go away. Just stay calm. It will go away." By March 24 over sixty thousand cases had been confirmed with multiple deaths, but Trump ignored the trend, stating, "I would love to have the country opened up and just raring to go by Easter." Demonstrating his complete ignorance of the pandemic and ignoring his own advisors, Trump declared that they were beginning to see the light at the end of the tunnel. As cases and deaths surged in the US, other government leaders such as VP Mike Pence, presidential advisor Jared Kushner, and several governors of Republican states, like Florida and South Dakota, all downplayed the virus. By the time the modern pandemic began to subside, there were over fifteen thousand deaths in Ontario alone and over a million in the United States; history seemed to be repeating itself.

By the end of September 1918, in the newly named city of Kitchener, the news rapidly changed from reporting that the city was free of any contagious diseases to declaring that the Spanish flu was invading the city. It wasn't long before the city had many cases of the virus, as hospitals began to fill up and health care providers worked long and arduous shifts addressing the needs of the inflicted. Public meetings were cancelled by the Board of

Health, and the Kitchener-Waterloo hospital was closed to visitors as doctors became overwhelmed.

On October 1, the *News Record* reported 250 cases and an initial death. The first victim in the area was a twenty-one-year-old woman who lived a short distance from the Metz's home on Benton Street. Industry in the region was also hit hard as factories like Kaufman Rubber, Merchants Rubber, and the Jackson and Cochrane foundry, shut down for a week as a precautionary measure. More deaths followed, and the virus spread rapidly in settings such as the Dominion Rubber Company, which experienced over 350 cases.

In the 2020 pandemic our experiences were similar, as large numbers of Covid occurrences were found in industries such as meatpacking,[19] and some workers died. In 1918, while cases continued to rise, the Ontario Provincial Board of Health, responding to a plea to close schools, theaters, and churches, advised against it. However, Kitchener's own Board of Health supervisor, Dr. Harry Lackner, objected to this opinion, saying, "He knows nothing about it. Let him come here and see the situation. Isolation with any disease is a splendid weapon."[20] By October 7, the Board of Health closed schools, theatres and churches indefinitely, as influenza was on the rise. Yet, even while the notice of closure appeared in the paper, the opinion that "the climax has been reached and in the next few days the epidemic should be on the wane"[21] was also expressed, and a notice appeared for a dance that week. Two hundred thousand cases were now reported in USA military camps, and locally, an isolation hospital was set up for the more serious cases.

As we know from our experience in the 2020 pandemic, controversies erupt. For example, in 1918, while schools, theatres and churches closed, poolrooms remained open. Additionally, resistance to the restrictions was commonplace. In one case, a celebration for the end of the war took place, led by a procession of two fire trucks sporting Allied flags, followed by the Boys Band and school children waving the Union Jack. At the band stand, people gathered and gave speeches brimming with enthusiasm for peace. School children sang patriotic songs, finishing with "God Save The King." In the recent pandemic, some groups and gatherings such as churches openly defied health mandates by holding services. The infamous President Trump was well known for contradicting his own government's recommendations by holding events such as the celebration of a new Supreme Court justice, which turned into a super spreader event.

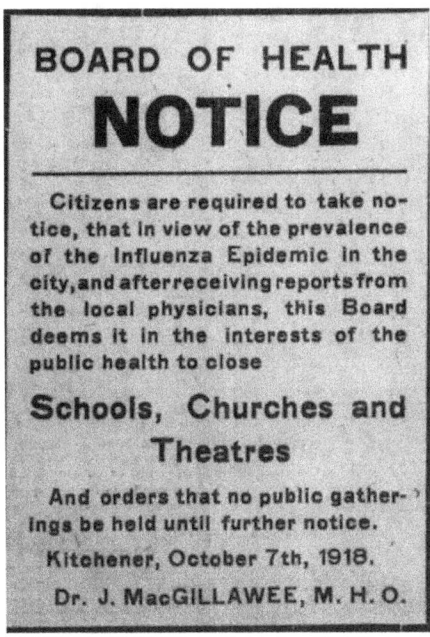

Notice in Local Paper, 1918

Trump was also known for his promotion of untested "cures" such as hydroxychloroquine. It was no different in 1918. As drug stores were busy filling prescriptions, citizens began to invent home remedies such as camphor gum and bone set tea. Self-appointed "pandemic experts" recommended a periodic bite from onion and garlic or peppermint candies. Other armchair authorities, maybe somewhat tongue-in-cheek, argued that cider and whiskey should be consumed in "liberal quantities" to ward off the influenza. While these homemade remedies mostly seemed harmless, we should remember that the USA President Trump pondered the use of bleach as a possible antidote to the Covid virus in 2020. Social media also spread innumerable remedies such as herbal teas, gargling with salt water, cow urine, horse medications for parasites, spiritual vaccines, garlic, boiled ginger, and anti-malarial drugs (again promoted by Trump).

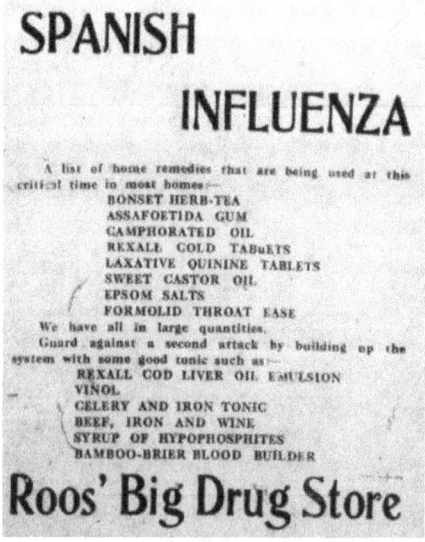

Notice in Local Paper, 1918

Then as now, the reporting on the pandemic was often conflicting. On October 10, 1918, the *News Record* wrote that "The weather seems a little more favourable again today, and with continued sunshine the epidemic should soon pass away," [22] reminiscent of Trump's claim that with warmer weather the virus would become weaker and go away.[23] Yet on the very same page, the *News Record* noted that "At present, doctors are not able to handle the situation. It's beyond our control … what we need in the worst way at present is an institution where the more serious cases of pneumonia can be isolated."[24] Additionally, the obituaries for that day reported at least seven deaths, with two young couples tragically leaving behind little children. Even the newspaper was not exempt, apologizing and warning that subscribers may experience delays or miss delivery entirely, as newsboys were becoming ill. As care centres filled, a shortage of medical personnel became a major concern. Nurses, who "must be secured and secured quickly," were recruited from other cities.

In the 2020 pandemic, as many hospital staff – especially ICU workers – experienced burnout, severe nurse shortages began to occur as well, and some provinces like Alberta Health Services (AHS) began to consider hiring outside contract personnel to cover staffing shortages. In both pandemics, the front-line workers were recognized for their contributions. The News Record acknowledged that the "young ladies from the factories were lauded for volunteering for nursing duty." Still, degrading others was not unusual, as some recently graduated nurses in the community were shamed for not stepping forward and lending a hand. In the 2020, we took to praising our health care workers with a seven o'clock balcony cheer every night. That cheer later gave way to bands of repulsive anti-maskers and anti-vaccine groups taking their protests to hospital grounds in several provinces.[25]

While there are striking similarities between the pandemics of 1918 and 2020, there are some notable differences. The earlier pandemic affected mostly younger persons between twenty and forty years of age, while the recent pandemic saw older persons, especially those in long-term care facilities, suffer the most. In 1918, little was known about viruses in general, and treatments were far less advanced. There was not much medical advice other than to isolate, wash your hands, cough into your sleeve, and no kissing. A vaccine did not exist, and the virus was not isolated until 1933. Moreover, the tragedies of the war such as dead and injured soldiers coming home provided a completely different backdrop to this pandemic.

Perhaps there are some lessons to take away from these experiences. In the time of the Napoleonic wars, Donald's grandparents were front row witnesses to the atrocities of war, and still they survived. They persisted through a long and arduous migration and settlement in a new country, and they endured. In the early part of the twentieth century, Donald's parents lived through another war in addition to a pandemic. Imagine the life of a family and their children; the news is reporting negotiations to finally end the war, there are still outbreaks of violence and skirmishes, soldiers, often wounded, are starting to return to their home communities, and a pandemic encompasses their world. And life still goes on.

As the country recovered and began to focus on rebuilding and moving forward, Aaron and Rosetta were starting their family. By the end of the pandemic, the couple had three sons: Floyd, Carl, and Ivan. They were now "roaring" into a revitalized bustling community with its greatest misfortunes in the rear-view mirror when the youngest of their four boys,

Donald James Metz, was born on December 12, 1922. Aaron and Rosetta each grew up in the aftermath of their parents' struggles, which included displacement, prejudice, immigration, war, and a plague. They survived and brought forth a strong work ethic and a bit of a rebellious nature, leaving the farm and establishing their home in the city. Life's most distressing struggles were behind them, and an exciting new world with innovations such as household electricity was emerging, and they were part of it. It seemed as if the young Donald would soon be able to join in a prosperous new environment without the struggles of his grandparents by his side.

Footnotes Chapter 4

[1] C.S. Lewis, best known for *The Chronicles of Narnia*, served and was injured in WWI.

[2] John English, and Kenneth McLaughlin, *Kitchener: An Illustrated History*, (Wilfred Laurier University Press, 1983): 86.

[3] William J. Campbell, "We Germans…are British Subjects. The First World War and the Curious Case of Berlin", *Canadian Military History*, 21, 2, (April 2015): 48.

[4] Campbell, "We Germans," 50.

[5] Campbell, "We Germans," 52.

[6] Cindy Day, "Anti-German Sentiment in Berlin During the First World War," Waterloo, ON:1988, p. 6, as quoted in Campbell, "We Germans."

[7] The Tory leader asserted that the measures imposed by his government in 2012 to deny special health care to people whose claim for refugee status had been denied were supported by new immigrants and "old-stock" Canadians alike. CBC https://www.cbc.ca/news/politics/canada-election-2015-harper-debate-1.3233785.

Footnotes cont'd

[8] Andrea Bellemare, "Ten facts about the mystery of the missing Kaiser's bust." *Social Sharing, CBC News*, posted August 22, 2014, https://www.cbc.ca/news/canada/kitchener-waterloo/10-facts-about-the-mystery-of-the-missing-kaiser-s-bust-1.2740729.

[9] George Floyd was brutally assaulted and murdered by police in Minneapolis on May 25, 2020.

[10] Tyler Stiem,, "What Should We Do With Troublesome Statues." *The Guardian*, Wednesday. Sept 8, 2018.
https://www.theguardian.com/cities/2018/sep/26/statue-wars-what-should-we-do-with-troublesome-monuments.

[11] Rych Mills, "Flash from the Past: Original Victoria Park pavilion was architectural beauty", *Waterloo Region Record*, February 20, 2015, https://www.waterloochronicle.ca/living-story/5347041-flash-from-the-past-original-victoria-park-pavilion-was-architectural-beauty

[12] For example see Lochead's personal papers and interpretive articles held by LCMSDS, "Local Support For The 118th," https://waterlooatwar.ca/2015/11/04/local-support-for-the-118th.

[13] Katie Rogers, "Boaty McBoatface: What You Get When You Let the Internet Decide," *New York Times*,
https://www.nytimes.com/2016/03/22/world/europe/boaty-mcboatface-what-you-get-when-you-let-the-internet-decide.html.

[14] Campbell, "We Germans," 45-57.

[15] Campbell, "We Germans," 45-57.

[16] *The Kitchener News Record*, July 9, 1918, p.4.

[17] *The News Record*, Sept 28, 1918, p.1.

[18] Kathryn Watson, "A timeline of what Trump has said on coronavirus." Updated on: April 3, 2020 / 6:35 pm / *CBS News*, https://www.cbsnews.com/news/timeline-president-donald-trump-changing-statements-on-coronavirus/.

Footnotes cont'd

[19] Joel Dryden, and Sarah Rieger, "New COVID-19 outbreak declared at Cargill meat plant in Alberta — site of Canada's largest outbreak", *CBC News* Posted: Feb 06, 2021 https://www.cbc.ca/news/canada/calgary/cargill-high-river-outbreak-1.5904444.

[20] *The Kitchener News Record*, Oct 10, 1918, 2.

[21] *The Kitchener News Record*, October 8, 1918, 7.

[22] *The Kitchener News Record*, October 10, 1918, 2.

[23] Wolfe, Daniel and Dale, Daniel, "'It's going to disappear': A timeline of Trump's claims that Covid-19 will vanish." *CNN*, https://www.cnn.com/interactive/2020/10/politics/covid-disappearing-trump-comment-tracker.

[24] *The Kitchener News Record*, Oct 10, 1918, 2.

[25] Bill Kaufmann, "Anti-vaccine protesters harassing health care workers, patients: AHS president," *Calgary Herald*, Sep 03, 2021.

Victoria News Staff, "Hundreds of anti-vaccine passport protesters rally outside B.C. legislature", *Victoria News*, Sept. 1, 2021, https://www.vicnews.com/news/hundreds-of-anti-vaccine-protestors-rally-outside-b-c-legislature.

Camille Bains, "Doctors frustrated with 'selfishness' of anti-vaccine protesters, people unvaccinated against COVID-19," *The Canadian Press*, September 3, 2021, https://www.theglobeandmail.com/canada/article-doctors-frustrated-with-selfishness-of-anti-vaccine-protesters.

Chapter 5

Society As Donald Enters The World

I shared their restlessness, understood their determination to free themselves of the Victorian shackles of the pre-World War I era and find out for themselves what life was all about.

– Colleen Moore

In trying to understand the values of another era, we can reflect on our own experiences, which may parallel the practices of another time. In the 2016 election in the United States, it is hard to imagine Trumpism as having any meaningful connection to society in the world my namesake uncle entered in the 1920s. In Trump's world, the irrationality of his disputing his electoral defeat in the 2020 United States election culminated in a storming of the Capitol building on January 6, 2021, as his supporters violently occupied the United States Congress. The riots claimed multiple lives in a protest that was viewed by some as an insurrection attempt. An attempt filled with wild rhetoric and outlandish absurdities. A widely shared tweet by Yousef Munayyer summed up the insurgency with the remark that "we spend $750 billion annually on 'defense' and the center of the American government fell in two hours to the *Duck Dynasty* and the guy in the Chewbacca bikini."[1]

Many of the perpetrators of the assault on the Capital were dressed in outlandish costumes. As ridiculous as these costumes may have been, they can reveal an ideology beneath the surface. Writer Elena Sheppard, in her remarks on the Capitol riot, argues that:

> *When we actually read the T-shirt slogans and interpret the symbols – especially given the history of groups like the Ku Klux Klan – what the Capitol insurrectionists wore becomes more consequential and a lot more menacing.*[2]

Generally speaking, it seems that the 1920s era was much more comparable to our 2020s than one might envision. During Trump's re-election campaign, another political commentator suggested that:

> *Donald Trump is running a campaign in 2020 that seems to come straight out of 1920, a time when the second incarnation of the KKK was at its height, a red scare was underway, there was much violence in the streets, and the attorney general was acting as a personal hatchet man for a president who disliked foreigners.*[3]

The dislike of foreigners in the 2020s also mirrored society from the 1920s. As the First World War ended, there was indeed a general fear that immigrants would remain loyal to their homelands. "Hyphenated" citizens, for example Japanese-Americans or Waterloo's German-Canadians, were the potential targets of racism, whether they held sympathies for their lands of origin or not. Donald was born near the end of 1922, and as he grew up in the shadow of his older brothers, he was confronted with a societal context that pitted the harsh realities of discrimination, gender inequalities, and a range of social inhibitions, such as prohibition, against the underlying current of a progressive and open-minded community.

At this time, various stories of racial discrimination and its brutal consequences could be easily found in the news. On the day of Donald's birth, it was reported that a posse captured a "negro" in a region of the United States where three negroes had already been burned to death by a mob several months ago. Even though the alleged victim, a white girl, failed to identify the captive as the assailant, hundreds of persons hurried to the scene to seek their brand of "justice" – a rope and a tree. Although the incident occurred in the United States, the fact that it was reported locally – along with comparable stories – illustrates the extensive nature of the problem.

In recent times, there have been daily riots in the streets because of the punishing death of George Floyd in the hands of the Minneapolis police. Riots, as well as a daily purge of racist statues, are taking place around the world even during a global pandemic. It seems that as I research the world into which Donald arrived that it is almost like yesterday. Following years of racial discrimination, especially at the hands of the police, George Floyd's death ignited a powerful response. In Donald's era, the case of Eugene Williams was no less sensational.

At the dawn of the second decade of the twentieth century, there was an extraordinary incident which fuelled historical grievances. Eugene Williams, a seventeen-year-old boy of colour, swam into a part of Lake Michigan that was designated for whites only. The teenage Williams was subsequently brutally stoned and drowned. Black people in Chicago took to the streets in protest and were attacked by white mobs, who destroyed homes and businesses on Chicago's south side. Police did nothing to protect the black population, and throughout what was called the Red Summer, riots took place all over the United States, resulting in numerous deaths and arrests of black protestors. Following the riots, the city convened a commission to study the causes of the violence. In an interview on the "Red Summer" given shortly after the death of George Floyd, renowned historian Khalil Gibran Muhammad stated:

> *And what comes out of that is the first blue-ribbon commission to study the causes of riots. In that report, the Chicago commission [concludes] that there was systemic participation in mob violence by the police, and that when police officers had the choice to protect black people from white mob violence, they chose to either aid and abet white mobs or to disarm black people or to arrest them. And a number of people testify, all of whom are white criminal justice officials, that the police are systematically engaging in racial bias when they're targeting black suspects, and more likely to arrest them and to book them on charges that they wouldn't do for a white man.[4]*

Sadly, aiding and abetting violent white mobs is reminiscent of the recent case of Kyle Rittenhouse in the summer of 2020. Following the shooting of a black man by a police officer in Kenosha, Wisconsin, the seventeen-year-old Rittenhouse shot and killed two persons participating in subsequent protest. Law enforcement officers were seen thanking and offering water to the armed civilians and militia groups who had taken to the streets against the demonstrators. In a controversial decision, Rittenhouse was later found not guilty of murder. In recent years, numerous cases have been documented of white vigilantes targeting, harming, and killing members of the black community. Khalil Gibran Muhammad concluded that the Chicago report assembled in 1922, the year of Donald's birth, "should have been the death of systemic police racism and discrimination in America. It wasn't. Its recommendations were largely ignored."

In the face of such a divide in the 1920s, the Ku Klux Klan experienced a resurgence as the perceived saviour of white American civilization. The film *Birth of a Nation*, based on the novel *The Clansman*, had been a commercial success, portraying African-Americans in a negative light while the Ku Klux Klan emerged as heroes. In the 1920s, fraternal community-based associations like the Masons, the Elks, and the Knights of Columbus became popular, and the Ku Klux Klan secured a position alongside such service groups, granting it a measure of respectability. The Klan grew to a membership of four million plus, and with their hooded regalia and "patriotic" flying of flags, they intimidated all who might oppose them. At the Democratic National Convention in 1924, delegates brought to the floor an anti-Klan measure to condemn the organization for its violence. The proposal was defeated. While the Klan claimed a foothold in the heartland of America, concern also began to be expressed in Canadian communities.

The radical American experience was not lost on Canadian citizens, and the news reported regularly on the unstable nature of American politics. As today, Canadians took a measured approach. On the day of Donald's birth in 1922, an opinion in the paper stated that "the Ku Klux Klan is said to be invading Canada. Let them uncover their faces and give people a chance to look them over."[5] While concern about the nature of the activities of the KKK was evident, it was not unusual for Canadians to be influenced by activities and policies percolating

Society As Donald Enters The World 69

in the United States. The Klan also held a significant position in the prohibition of alcohol. The restriction of alcohol was also in effect in Ontario from 1916 to 1927. Prohibition was not just a skirmish between teetotalers and imbibers. In the United States and Canada, a battle over booze could be raged violently. It was reported in the *Kitchener Record*, on the day Donald was born, that:

> *Preparations to mass 500 prohibition agents, equipped with bombing planes and machine guns for an onslaught on the mountain stronghold of Bob Ballard's band of moonshiners, are being made by United States federal authorities ... pointing out that only by bombing the entire mountain would it be possible to drive the moonshiners from their caves.*[6]

The prohibition era in Canada was arguably driven by pious religious groups, and in the midst of the Mennonite enclave of Kitchener-Waterloo, one would have expected the debate to be robustly opposed to alcohol. However, the discourse seemed much more composed, and the consumption of beer was used as a wedge against the so called evils of imbibing liquor.

> *We believe there is hardly one man in a hundred who desires the return of whiskey for sale in the hotel bar. But there are many non-drinking men who do not believe it should be made entirely impossible to obtain a light beer for use in moderation, without violation of the law.*[7]

This view reflects my own personal experience. A few years ago I was hosting a high school principal from a school I worked with in Costa Rica. I wanted him to visit a variety of educational institutions in our community, so we went to a public school, a private school, and a school on a nearby Mennonite colony. The elder who graciously received us at the colony described life on the colony to my guest. The elder was adamant that, contrary to some popular opinion of Mennonites, alcohol consumption was not prohibited, especially after a hard day's labour on the farm. Anecdotally, I sometimes purchased alcohol at a nearby liquor store, and it was not uncommon to see a colony truck parked outside on a Friday night with a few of the men patronizing the store and even occasionally enjoying their "post farming" drink in the parking lot.

The notion of consuming a "light" beer in moderation was quickly adopted by breweries in the waning days of prohibition. The marketing of beer products was disassociated from saloons and drunkenness, gambling and prostitution, and most certainly had an influence on the young Donald while he negotiated his teenage years. He took up drinking beer enthusiastically.

It is not hard for us today to relate to the liberalization of alcohol consumption as we face the legalization of cannabis. Recently, the typical arguments of social decline and moral corruption of smoking cannabis have given way to the practical questions of how far away from schools will liquor/cannabis outlets be permitted. Regardless of the pro or contra arguments for prohibition, the reality is simply that prohibition did not work, in either case, one hundred years apart. Even though illegal for decades, everyone seems to know how to buy marijuana even if they do not use it (ask any high school student). A similar tongue-in-cheek sentiment could be found in the 1920s, as reported locally in the *Elmira Siguet*: "Police are hunting bootleggers, most everybody else seems to have found theirs."[8]

As Donald started to walk the streets, Canadians saw themselves as significantly more reasonable with regard to the societal issues than their southern neighbours. However, not all could escape the rhetoric and practice of systemic racism. The current cultural struggles in the United States mirror conflicts that involved the fear that immigrants or refugees were here to steal our jobs. For example, in the 1920s, Thomas More, a board member of the Canadian National Railway, was chastised in the newspaper for his views on the total exclusion of immigrants. "He has even been fearful that if men were admitted as farmers they might ultimately drift into the towns and cities and become factors in the labour market."[9] Many Canadians also struggled with the treatment of Indigenous persons at this time. In a description of "white man's" justice, a RCMP officer in the far north, investigating the murder of a white trader, performed all the duties of a constable, coroner, and magistrate. He conducted the investigation, performed the autopsy, issued warrants, presided over the preliminary enquiry, and committed three Indigenous males to stand trial.[10]

Another noteworthy influence in the social fabric of the time was gender inequality. Women who were part of the war effort received the vote in 1916; eventually in the post-war period, all women received the right to vote. Further progress for women would prove to be a lifetime challenge, as the men were expected to be men. Donald did not escape these cultural norms while growing up in a patriarchal society which struggled to attain any degree of gender equality. The job advertisements in the paper focused on tasks for men such as a cabinet maker, farm workers (specifically for a married man), night fireman, and general labourers. For women, a limited number of ads were for housekeepers, maids, and the odd time for a stenographer or sewing machine operator. In their letters to Santa, girls asked for dolls and a carriage, a set of dishes, or a purse; while little boys wanted model building sets or a picture machine.

It was also not hard to hear or find a sexist rant often printed right in the local paper's "joke" column. On the day of Donald's birth, we find the following gems:

> *"About all some girls know about a needle is that one has to change it after each record."*
>
> *"I am so glad you smoke a pipe said the bride. It gives you such a nice man taste."*[11]

The young Donald was also taught how to engage with a lady "thoughtfully." For example, as electrical distribution rapidly expanded, electrical appliances made their way into the home with the promotion of labour-saving devices for women that would "elevate the status of homemakers." [12] Donald, his brothers, and male friends were initiated into the proper way to treat a lady by newspaper advertisements that clearly illustrated the "thoughtfulness" of a man buying his spouse a Christmas gift:

> *For, this year, it had to be a worth-while gift – something that mother would be proud to show her friends. A Royal Electric Cleaner was dad's happy solution of the problem. Did mother really want her Royal? Well, rather! – Secretly she had longed for the superior features of the royal – it was just the cleaner she hoped to find – but she had hardly dared expect that one would be hers so soon. Yet there it was, thanks to dad's and the children's thoughtfulness, – ready at her bidding to make housecleaning easier for her thru all the days to come.*[13]

Of course, it was the men who were concerned about making "woman's work" much more appealing! Donald grew up in this environment, inside a patriarchal household with a loving mother who tended to her boys. While many young men in these surroundings were dedicated to their mothers, they still struggled to grasp the gender norms of equality, and what that truly meant.

To engage young boys and men in such conversations still remains a challenge today. Even though we would like to view ourselves as advancing rapidly towards gender equality, the reality remains that we have a long road ahead in dealing with contradictory attitudes. On one hand, we see more women entering positions of power in government, but their colleagues still often demean their authority and contributions. Hillary Margolis points out the myriad of sexist remarks that political leaders around the world unabashedly express. In reference to the United States President Trump's infamous remark on using his manly power to grab women "by the p***y," the United Kingdom Independence Party (UKIP) and Brexit leader Nigel Farage brushed it off as "alpha male boasting ... that men do."[14] Another member of the UKIP party joined in the gender bashing in tweeting a request to silence Scottish Prime Minister Nicola Sturgeon by "taping her mouth shut," adding, "and her legs, so she can't reproduce."[15]

Even today, Canada does not escape this routine. Michelle Rempel, a federal Conservative member of Parliament, outlined the everyday sexism she confronts in being called the "bitch" epithet. The reference is often found in comments by her male colleagues, who have suggested she address their issue when "she becomes less emotional." Rempel also noted she experiences taunts when she – or any other woman – does not readily obey a male's request or yield to his position on an issue.

They are faced with comments such as "that I have gotten to my station in life by (insert your choice of sexual act) with (insert your choice of man in position of authority)." Rempel argues, women are subjected to "commentary that links my appearance to my competency" or behaviour that "involves my ass being occasionally grabbed as a way to shock me into submission."[16] Indeed, the road is long.

As I consider the context in which Donald was raised, I certainly would be remiss not to emphasize that progress in combating societal norms such as gender inequality can be a slow and arduous journey. However, even though Donald lived in a sphere that was challenged by racial discrimination, systemic gender inequality, and the moral enforcement of a pious community, progressive ideas were also starting to emerge as a challenge to the status quo. In several cases, some opinions in the local paper could be rather progressive. For example, one writer, obviously familiar with the norms of Scandinavian countries, argued against the incarceration of juveniles and sending boys to a penitentiary with adults. In a reference to Norway, he stated that:

> *Once a youth goes to prison the odds are strongly against his ever running straight. He comes in contact with the worst kinds of criminals. In Canada, we still occasionally send boys of sixteen to penitentiary; to our shame it be said… Canadians generally pride themselves to be in far advance of the European countries, in some things we have a good deal to learn from them.*[17]

And concerning children born out of wedlock, certainly a shame in a pious community, the writer noted that:

> *Norway treats legitimate and illegitimate children alike, believing that the latter are not to blame for the indiscretions of their parents ... they do not punish or ostracize the innocent.[18]*

Naturally, all children are innocent. As Donald started his journey as a young boy, the indiscriminate behaviours of the time were an aside to being a child. Family was central in protecting this innocence, however, as Patrick Rothfuss reminds us, "The day we fret about the future is the day we leave our childhood behind."[19] For a child, concern about the future frequently begins with death. When his time came, Donald's grandfather, Reinhardt, passed away in the family home with his daughter and grandchildren at his side. Donald was just six years old; his paternal grandfather had died many years earlier, so Donald grew up not knowing both of his grandfathers. A situation that is easy for me to relate to, as I never knew either of my grandfathers as well. Grandfathers can play a number of roles in a young boy's childhood, roles that embody their aged wisdom and experience. They are often mentors, coaches, or a friend who offers a patient ear in the face of parental frustration. I am reminded of the words of the song "Grandfather" by the renowned Canadian entertainer and master story-teller Winston Wuttunnee:

> *Your words are strong, they tell me where I belong*
> *And the picture you have painted with your ancient memory*
> *Are the pictures that will set my children free[20]*

There is a childhood innocence grandfathers both protect and help us understand. Grandfathers have all kinds of stories to tell, you can make memories with them that last a lifetime, and in them you have a role model when it's your turn to grandparent.

For Donald and other children in his time, it was not unusual to lose your grandparents at an early age. When you have no grandfathers, and your father works sixty hours a week, young boys often turned to their close male friends for companionship and guidance. The complications of societal norms were always easier to traverse with a good pal by your side.

The young Donald grew up on Benton Street in Kitchener, Ontario, where he became close friends with a boy around the corner on Mill Street, Mel Howey. Donald's brother Carl, whose best friend was Mel's brother Wilf Howey, were all close in age, and the group always made for a rollicking time and enduring friendship. One of the boys' favourite places to play was Victoria Park, only a few blocks from their home. Victoria Park was a popular venue for residents to gather. Even those "out of towners" from the nearby communities of Waterloo, Preston, and Galt enjoyed the park's recreational scene so much that a railway platform was built on the edge of the park. A huge pavilion was also constructed in the park to accommodate community picnics and would often be used for events by companies, churches, and schools. For Donald, his brothers, and his friends, Victoria Park was a home away from home. In winter, the park was the place to go ice skating, in summer it was baseball. Even though the ice was often only four inches thick, thousands of citizens flocked to the park from freeze-up in December to spring thaw.

The park was also the location used by commercial ice-cutters, and when efforts were made to expand the skating areas, a conflict emerged between the recreational and economic uses of the park. A persuasive argument was made that the health and recreation of the young skaters was more important than ice-cutting.[21] Soon electricity would side with the youth, as the modern refrigerator reduced the need for ice boxes.

Donald would experience the onset of a host of new and innovative technologies that were becoming available to a wider audience. Electricity was the main driving force behind these new inventions. In the subsequent decades, society and home life transformed dramatically as electrical distribution became widely available. Electricity, which today we take for granted, was a revolutionary experience for everyone in the early decades of the twentieth century.

There is no doubt, as I consider the context in which Donald grew up, that I can easily identify with his world. The dawn of the electric age is not very different to our own historic transformation beginning in the late 20th century with the emergence of the digital age. We have experienced a rapid change from traditional industry and modes of life to one that is dominated by information technology. Some of the shift, for example, the advent of micro-computers, is readily apparent. Electronic gadgets, such as multi-purpose mobile devices like iPods, changed the way we obtained and listened to music. Later tablets, smart phones, and apps changed the way we met, worked, and played. We now have a wealth of knowledge, confounded by misinformation, at our fingertips, and everyone has become an expert on social media.

The age of electricity was no less dramatic, as the natural environment changed rapidly. In our time, cell phone towers and satellites emerged, while Donald and his family faced the erection of hydro poles and transmission wires. The arrival of new technologies always has some adverse effects that we must deal with in ways never imagined. Substantial changes to the local landscape, such as the construction of hydro poles and swinging wires, may seem quite inoffensive today. However, some people initially viewed these as wretched eyesores, while others considered them simply as an inconvenience that the innovations mandated. Moreover, each innovation introduced a new hazard. For example, electric street lights first replaced the cumbersome gas lights in the more affluent parts of town. The brightly lit areas then marked the difference between wealthy residents and the poor ones, who now resided in older, shadowy neighbourhoods. Crime naturally progressed into the dimly lit sections of town.

The advent of electric streetcars was another example of a "convenience" that introduced new challenges to their users. In her studies, Dorotea Gucciardo notes that

"Pedestrians were being struck, passengers were sometimes falling out of running trams or injured after an abrupt stop, and numerous automobiles collided with streetcars."[22]

In an effort to avoid accidental deaths, especially among children, politicians ultimately enacted a strict no jaywalking law.

Electrical hazards were now also found in the home that could cause electrocution and death. Even today, we experience more than three hundred electrocution deaths and four thousand injuries each year in North America. But as electricity in the home became a desirable commodity, the infrastructure and the associated perils soon merged into everyday life. The advent of a new age of electricity also led a revolution in communications, with the telephone and radio leading the way. Just as I have lived through the advancement of the computer, Donald experienced the evolution of radio – from a curious innovation at the beginning of the 1920s to a widely popular medium by the early 1940s. Radio proved to be much more captivating than reading newspaper accounts, especially for entertainment like comedy and hockey games. Ironically, the first radio hockey broadcast by the renowned Foster Hewitt was a game between the Toronto Argonauts and the Kitchener Greenshirts, when Foster coined the iconic phrase "he shoots, he scores!"[23] Donald's favourite team was the Greenshirts, who played out of the Kitchener Auditorium, where he was a well-known ice scraper in the 1940s. In the 1930s, Donald, like me much later, became accustomed to Hewitt's infamous greeting of "Hello Canada and hockey fans in the United States and Newfoundland."

The telephone was another innovation that saw a meteoric ascent. The phone call opened regular communications with persons outside of your own household, and permitted people, especially young adults, to connect easily with their friends. For Donald, it was an effortless way to gather his pals for a weekend rendezvous at the park or a meet-up at the dance hall. While the telephone unlocked the circle of communications, and electric streetcars extended individual modes of travel, inter-personal connections grew quickly. You could now be in touch with your friends by telephone and move rapidly from one part of the city to another. For most young people, this expanded their entertainment and employment possibilities. Electricity enabled assembly lines and shift work just as more individuals were attracted to urban areas away from the farm. As the electricity age evolved, more demand for new skills emerged, and the need for an educated population kept young people in school longer. A brand-new culture for youth began to emerge.

As is the case with most new technologies, there was also a seedy component constantly trying to take advantage of an unsuspecting public, especially young people. Today, in the digital age, foreign princes claim to hold massive fortunes for us in return for an upfront fee, internet users can easily download pornography, sexual predators troll to identify potential victims online, and misinformation is deliberately disseminated to muddy the political landscape and influence elections. In Donald's world, "marvellous" new inventions such as electric vibrators were marketed as cure-alls. One ad in the magazine *Popular Mechanics* claimed:

> *Even if you have a chronic disease – one that physicians have told you is incurable ... NOW AT YOUR COMMAND! VIBRATION – Banishes disease as the sun banishes mist!* [24]

This new electric vibrator claimed it could cure headaches, rheumatism, constipation, baldness, and deafness, among other things. Although strict advertising regulations at this time would never permit erotic claims, a new "sex toy" was definitely on the table.[25]

In reflecting on the world my uncle grew up in, many might feel we had little in common. However, I can easily identify with his changing world and the influence of innovative technologies, societal norms, and prejudices. It was a new and exciting world, with many new and exciting possibilities. In addition, numerous challenges and temptations were placed in the way. Donald, growing up in a rapidly changing environment, waltzed into another significant cultural transformation: the emergence of the teenager.

Footnotes Chapter 5

[1] Munayyer, Yousef. @YousefMunayyer, Twitter: 7:44 PM · Jan 6, 2021, https://twitter.com/yousefmunayyer/status/1347026407294201863?lang=en.

Footnotes cont'd

[2] Elena Sheppard, "Pro-Trump Capitol rioters like the 'QAnon Shaman' looked ridiculous — by design," *THINK: Opinion, Analysis, Essays*, https://www.nbcnews.com/think/opinion/pro-trump-capitol-rioters-qanon-shaman-looked-ridiculous-design-ncna1254010.

[3] Bates, Christopher, "Democrats Smell Blood in the Water," July 7, 2020, https://electoral-vote.com.

[4] Anna North, "How racist policing took over American cities, explained by a historian", *Vox*, https://ww.vox.com/2020/6/6/21280643/police-brutality-violence-protests-racism-khalil-muhammad.

[5] *Kitchener Record*, Dec 12, 1922.

[6] *Kitchener Record*, Dec 12, 1922.

[7] *Kitchener Record*, Dec 12, 1922.

[8] Robert J. Bonds and William C. Mattys, *Elmira Siguet*, 1925, as reported in the *Canadiana Scrapbook, The Confident Years: Canada in the 1920s*, p.7.

[9] *Kitchener Record*, Dec 11, 1922.

[10] *Kitchener Record*, Dec 13, 1922.

[11] *Kitchener Record*, Dec 13, 1922.

[12] Dorotea Gucciardo, "The Powered Generation: Canadians, Electricity, and Everyday Life", Electronic Thesis and Dissertation Repository. 258, 2011: 137.

[13] *Kitchener Record*, Dec 11, 1922.

[14] Hilary Margolis, "17 Times Politicians Resorted to Wildly Sexist Speech Over the Last Year," *New York Times*, March 13, 2017. https://www.hrw.org/news/2017/03/13/17-times-politicians-have-resorted-wildly-sexist-speech-over-last-year.

Footnotes cont'd

[15] Margolis, "17 Times."

[16] Michelle Rempel, "Confront your sexism." *National Post*, Apr 18, 2016, https://nationalpost.com/opinion/michelle-rempel- confront-your-sexism.

[17] *Kitchener Record*, Dec 11, 1922.

[18] *Kitchener Record*, Dec 11, 1922.

[19] Patrick Rothfuss, "The Name of the Wind: The Kingkiller Chronicles," (Hachette UK, 2007):73.

[20] Winston Wuttenee, Grandfather, YouTube video, https://www.youtube.com/watch?v=s2Z0tAyZBOQ.

[21] *Kitchener Record*, Dec 12, 1922.

[22] Gucciardo, "The Powered Generation," 67.

[23] David Zarum, "Hockey Night in Canada", *The Canadian Encyclopedia* (2019) www.thecanadianencyclopedia.ca/en/article/hockey-night-in-canada.

[24] Popular Mechanics, January 1909, p.145.

[25] Hallie Lieberman, "Selling Sex Toys: Marketing and the Meaning of Vibrators in Early Twentieth-Century America", *Enterprise and Society*, 17, no. 2 (June 2016): 393-433.

Chapter 6

Navigating The Teen Years

Parents can only give good advice or put them on the right paths, but the final forming of a person's character lies in their own hands.

— Anne Frank

Growing up in the 1930s became a unique challenge for the now eight-year-old Donald. The Great Depression defined the decade with a sharp decline in employment opportunities for men. By 1933, unemployment rose to almost thirty percent, and large numbers of Canadians were surviving on next to nothing, or meagre government assistance. Millions of Canadians were unemployed and hungry, and many were homeless. Exports plummeted, and severe drought in the prairies created a dust bowl known as the "dirty thirties." The country was engulfed in a transformation, and social welfare emerged as the government took a more active role in the country's economy.

The economy was not the only crisis facing the world; war clouds appeared over Germany as Jewish citizens were stripped of their civil rights, and Hitler and Mussolini emerged as leaders in their respective countries. Those tensions seemed distant at the time, but in the years to come they developed into a global menace.

In today's pandemic era, North American students leaving school – by graduating or otherwise – stumble into a world where hundreds of thousands have died of the Covid virus, countless businesses, such as restaurants and hospitality venues, have dissolved, and millions of persons have lost their employment and means of living. There is little doubt that young people of this age will have lost a degree of earning power, and these memories will follow them as they search for a role in a prosperous civilization. Many have lived in their parents' basements well beyond their dreams, and establishing meaningful relationships became a challenging endeavour in an era of masking and social distancing. As their social circles became compressed with home isolation mandates, many young people turned to their smart phones and online dating sites to rapidly expand their social reach, and that trend has continued. They imagine themselves with an unknown partner while swiping left or right on their apps in a routine with no real personal connection. With such a simple task, it is easy to become lost in the process. Many of the "swipers" struggle when the time arrives to establish a sincere relationship in person.

In this context, it is not difficult to relate to Donald's transition into the labour force and the adult world amid an economic depression. Young persons, like Donald, were beginning to emerge as a new crowd – the teenagers. They were transitioning from being controlled by their parents at home to expanding their social circles with their peers. This emerging culture was enabled by modern technologies such as the home telephone and accessible transportation, which were quickly embraced by Donald's generation. However, an awkwardness permeated this new process of transitioning from a strict home environment to more liberal outside personal contact, especially with the opposite sex.

The label "teenager" was initially coined in a book by Lawrence Augustus Averill: *Adolescence: A Study in the Teen Years in 1936*. In that year, Donald was fourteen years old. Commonly, young people were considered children who stepped into the world of adulthood when they left school, got a job, or got married. At the dawn of the 20th century, more adolescents were staying in school, especially in secondary education. The high school effectively became a lively meeting place, the center of new adolescent social experiences. The kids began to establish their own norms in terms of dress, jargon, recreation, and behaviours such as smoking, drinking, and sexual activity. The teens started to look to each other socially, rather than to their own parents, as they navigated a brand new transitional period between childhood and adulthood. Even though they lacked widespread acknowledgement, the teenagers were very much part of the scene by the close of the 1920s and into the 1930s.

At various times, teen expectations seemed conflicted, especially for teenage girls. For young women, "expert opinion held that true adult status still signified motherhood."[1] Donald's mother was nineteen when she married his father, while his grandmothers were sixteen and seventeen when they married their respective spouses. Both of Donald's grandmothers had eleven children. A woman's role was very clearly defined as motherhood and home management. Cynthia Comacchio, in her writings on the adolescent development of young women, summed up that at this time, "a modernized motherhood was the woman's badge of citizenship."[2] The emerging teenage culture was especially challenging for these young women, as new opportunities in education, employment, and personal lifestyles conflicted with the deep-rooted burdens of a 19th century paternalistic society. A young woman's struggle to achieve independence and self-determination was only just beginning and continues to this day. Even though many believe that tremendous steps have been made in women's liberation, young women still experience an extensive range of expectations and challenges in life and motherhood, including navigating work as a single parent, daycare accessibility, and mothering in an LGBTQ+ hesitant world.

Through Donald's teenage years, gender stereotypes were commonly reflected in the employment opportunities advertised for young women in the local paper. The few want ads addressing females focused on the tasks of housekeeping, cleaning, sewing, and occasionally clerical work. Teaching and nursing were also female-oriented occupations, but low wages, long hours, and personal restrictions, especially for single female schoolteachers, were the norm.

Additionally, women were often the brunt of social criticism for being employed, thus neglecting their household duties. Social commentators were "alarmed by the girl of the new day, whose appearance and demeanour made her a visible affront to middle-class domestic ideals."[3] In her discussion of societal expectations of the time, Veronica Strong-Boar summarizes a young girl's future:

> *Film, radio, newspapers, and magazines assured girls that "you are in a Beauty contest every day of Your Life." Marriage was the ultimate prize. "Little Mother" classes joined homemaking badges in Girl Guides and lecture in Canadian Girls in Training (CGIT) to encourage girls to assume domestic duties.[4]*

While no one would object to homemaking skills for any gender, the perception of "girls in training" established the assumptions and expectations that young women had to confront daily. Yet, she persisted; young women began to question the conventional wisdom on what constituted good behaviours. By the 1930s, many of the cultural changes brought about in the Roaring Twenties, such as movies, cars, radios, booze, flappers, and dance halls, were pursued by a teenage crowd in the new free time they now enjoyed.

While the emergence of a new teenage culture provided an exciting experience for many youths, it did not come without scrutiny. As many teens in the 1930s left school and failed to find employment, they were called out publicly in some newspapers and opinion columns for an emerging concern over juvenile delinquency. One of the most popular movies in the late 1930s was *Boys Town*, which depicted Father Flanagan (Spencer Tracey) starting a new orphanage for delinquent boys, countering the predisposition that young wayward boys should be locked up like men in prisons.

Correspondingly, teenage girls did not escape the critical eye of paternalism. Young women who embraced the modern style, especially those who adopted the "manly" habits of public smoking and drinking that often accompanied it, set off warning bells about the decline of "womanliness."[5]

Although some young women took up the unsavoury habits of smoking and drinking, one of the most loved new pastimes for teenage girls was dancing. Dance halls began to appear, and the Friday night dance became a mainstay in community clubs across the country. While many lamented the "decline of womanliness" and the spectre of juvenile delinquency, the girls fought back. In a letter to the editor of a newspaper, one teenage girl asked, "We would honestly like someone to tell us what is wrong with jitterbug dancing that makes you feel called upon to classify it with crime and juvenile delinquency."6

The girls loved to dance, much to the dismay of young men like Donald. He longed for female companionship but struggled with their aspirations. Donald was a regular at the local Granite Club, often going skating in the wintertime and attending the weekly dance. Shortly after a nineteen-year-old Donald joined the service, he wistfully wrote to his friend Mel about his predictable adventures at the dance hall. "After the skating we went to the dance as usual and went home alone."7 At his post in Brantford in 1942, he told Mel that the situation had not changed much for him. "Down here we haven't got a chance to get a woman because we don't dance and all the women do."8 The girls rejoiced in their new-found freedom to let loose and dance while the boys guarded the sidelines – perhaps swiping left and right in their imaginations.

The immense changes in the 1930s such as improvements in transportation, along with the advent of electricity and modern innovations, brought about extended free time and new social options for the emerging teen culture. Teens began to escape the watchful eyes of their parents, especially with respect to their social lives and dating. They expanded their personal privacies avoiding the direct supervision of mom and dad. The kids began ritual experimentation with contemporary vices such as smoking, drinking, and heightened sexual activity. There were now "cool kids", and Donald was definitely not one of the cool kids. He was a lonely wallflower at the dances and he lingered on the sidelines, though his friend Mel always had a way with the girls. Mel was Donald's best friend, and Donald became the ultimate wingman for Mel and his lady friends. At times, Donald would chastise his buddy to behave himself and treat the girls nice: "You know what happens at the end of the night – you don't talk to them anymore and I have to take care of them." [9] Donald always wanted to know if Mel's current girlfriend had any friends for him, and he often took a dig at Mel's tastes, once sarcastically asking if "she's an old whore or a respectable whore?"[10]

For Donald, like many young men, it was his close male companions and brothers that he related to the easiest. Neil Sutherland highlights the feelings of a young man in this time:

Part of the feeling was that I was now – A Man. It was pretty hard work but you had to prove that you were able to do something like that to be accepted by your peers, those who were a bit older than you.[11]

In the Depression era, many young males felt as if they were a burden to their families, ashamed of their unemployment and poverty. Many left their homes to wander about the country, often by jumping on rail cars. Still, the young men found ways to amuse themselves and an activity gaining popularity during the Depression was gambling. In the early part of the 20th century, gambling was mostly illegal, but pervasive. As the economy sagged, gambling laws were relaxed in some forms, including bingo, to enable organizations such as churches a means of raising funds. In 1931, the state of Nevada legalized most forms of gambling to secure a source of revenue for the state. To this day, the city of Las Vegas remains the hub of gambling in America.

Betting on horse racing and games such as playing cards, dice, and numbers became popular, and young men like Donald participated routinely with their friends, as a social activity. In gambling, men often assume the role of the alpha male:

asserting their authority, demonstrating risk and skill, and overcoming adversity. However, in defeat they could find depression and angst. Gambling could be a roller coaster, and Donald rode the highs and lows. He revelled in the highs, one time sending his mother a money order for $20 ($350 in today's currency), asking her to cash it and save it for him. He told his mom he won the money in a craps game. The letter illustrates Donald's close relationship with his mother, who tolerated his unpleasant habits and always remained by his side, even serving as his faithful confidante through their regularly exchanged correspondences.

But as Donald celebrated his gambling achievements, he also discovered that it was just as easy to lose your entire paycheque. At one point in his early training Donald wrote Mel, who also enjoyed the games, to tell him that "I just got out of a card game down $2.50 so I'm about the same as you."[12] Donald noted that if you played dice, it would cost $5 just to get in the game, and that he was going to give it up. While reckless at times with his gambling, Donald also seemed to maintain some semblance of common sense. Maybe he was encouraged by his mother when he advised Mel to join him in quitting gambling, in order to save their money for Christmas and New Year's.

Donald was also attracted to winter sports, keeping a pair of skis in the closet and a pair of skates at his side, both as a teenager and throughout his service. When not skating or playing hockey at Victoria Park, he could be found down the street at the Queen Street Auditorium known as the "Aud". A ten-minute walk from Donald's house on Benton Street, the Aud was initially built in 1904 with a natural ice surface. Artificial ice was installed with the refrigeration unit supplied by Silverwood Dairies in 1927. The skating arena quickly became the center for hockey enthusiasts in the area, hosting hockey teams like the Waterloo Siskins and the Kitchener Greenshirts.

On his death, it was reported in the paper that Donald "was well known at the auditorium, particularly as an ice scraper"[13] ... in common vernacular, a rink rat. A rink rat was usually a young man who always helped with cleaning the ice, sweeping, and light maintenance work, frequently without pay. However, it often resulted in free admission to the rink, where Donald was a huge admirer of the local hockey teams. Upon his death, in his kit bag (at that time in England), Donald still carried a pair of skates. Even though the opportunity for skating overseas was rare, the skates always stayed by his side.

One of the home teams at the auditorium in Donald's tenure as an ice scraper was the Kitchener Greenshirts, a junior hockey team in the Ontario Hockey Association. Members of this team from 1934–1936 included the famous "Kraut line," and Donald was a big follower. The Kraut line consisted of center Milt Schmidt and his wingers, Bobby Bauer and Woody Dumart. Milt Schmidt lived about a fifteen-minute walk west of the Queen Street Auditorium, and Milt maintained that "it was home to me and it was a palace, as far as I was concerned."[14]

Donald lived only ten minutes south of the Queen Street Auditorium, and as a young teenaged ice scraper at the Aud, he found himself watching Milt on a regular basis. Although Milt was four years older than Donald, and they never associated with each other, Donald was without question a super fan of Milt.[15] Donald's old brother Carl knew Marie Petersen, who would later become Milt's wife, and Milt was well known locally for his antics, such as fighting the boys at the Catholic elementary school in the neighbourhood.

Milt Schmidt also started his association with the Aud as a rink rat, selling peanuts for five cents a bag. He would arrive early on game days and help the players by carrying their sticks and skates.[16] Milt outlined the feeling towards hockey in the his old neighbourhood:

We wouldn't leave the house without bringing brooms and shovels with our skates to get the ice ready ... Boy, I am telling you what we went through to play. I think we deserved a medal of honor. But you know, it was worth it.[17]

Milt Schmidt was the role model Donald needed, and he often followed a parallel path to his hero. He kept right in tune with his idol – it did not matter how well he could play the game, Donald was always going to be a part of it; he earned his keep, inspired by Milt, with a shovel and a broom. Donald, at thirteen years of age, and a fixture at the ice rink, was a disciple of the 1934–35 Kitchener Greenshirts led by Milt and the Kraut line.

Milt, never a great student, dropped out of school at the age of fourteen and worked in a low paying job in a shoe factory. Ultimately, he pursued a stellar career in the National Hockey League, being elected to the Hockey Hall of Fame in 1961. Schmidt, Bauer, and Dumart all went on to play in the National Hockey League, but their tenure was interrupted by the war: all three enlisted in 1942. Schmidt, in the middle of his hockey career, spent three years overseas.

Donald, perhaps wishing to follow in the footsteps of his local hero, also quit school at fourteen and took a low paying job as a treer in a shoe factory. Donald never had the skills of an accomplished hockey player, but a few months after Schmidt enlisted in the service, Donald followed suit, though it was his second attempt. Donald first tried to enlist as an eighteen-year-old in September of 1941 and was turned down. He enlisted, as Milt did, in 1942.

The Queen Street Aud was home to many other sporting events that attracted the interests of young men, especially the rink rats. I get the psyche of my uncle and his preoccupation with the Aud. As a young lad of ten years, I followed my uncle's footsteps as a rink rat in the new Auditorium. I would play a game of hockey with my peewee team, then spend a few hours banging sticks with the other rats in any space we could find. After, we would sneak into the Greenshirts practice and watch our heroes play.

In my reflections over the years about my namesake uncle, I would often contemplate whether we had shared common experiences. As I researched events at the Queen Street Aud, I discovered that Whipper Billy Watson had pinned Joe Cox to the mat in a match in 1940. At this time, Watson was a young upcoming wrestler, and it is quite likely that Donald, with his rink rat status, was in the crowd. Twenty-five years later, as a young boy, I marvelled at Watson's immense size and strength when I stood beside him after a wrestling match on the main floor at the Kitchener Auditorium. I ponder from time to time about this improbable connection that I might have had with my uncle – it was the only wrestling match I ever attended in my life.

Another fun pastime for the teenage Donald and his best friend Mel was horseshoes. They maintained a pit in the yard and took on all comers. Caught up in the excitement of the game, they bet on their prowess, and they must have been good. In the Army, Mel served in the 1st Canadian Wireless Group, Royal Canadian Corps of Signals, and became the editor-in-chief of the Static Press, the group's newsletter. When he was stationed in Australia near the end of the war, the highlight of his group's sporting events was a horseshoe pitching duel, which took place in Brisbane. Mel Howey undoubtedly was a "ringer," as he easily became the unit champion by suffering no defeats throughout the tournament.

In 1937, Donald finished his grade nine studies at St. Jerome College.[18] Compulsory education was introduced in Ontario in 1871 for children between the ages of seven and twelve years of age. In 1921, the age was increased to sixteen, unless the student was excused by obtaining an employment certificate signed by their parents. School was no longer a consideration for young Donald once he reached fourteen, and he obtained his early release. Supported by his mother, he moved into the real world. I can easily relate to his situation: at seventeen, I left school for the first time and headed out on my own with the hope of finding my true self, where I fit in, and how I wanted to live my own life. I basically had no marketable skills; however, my work ethic drove me not to rest idly but take whatever came along and make the most of it.

Donald found employment, soon after leaving school, as a shoe treer at the Ontario Shoe Company. Unskilled labour meant low wages, and Donald left the company after only one year to become a "springer" at the DeLuxe Upholstering Company. Installing springs in furniture frames kept Donald occupied for three more years as he lived at home and pursued his recreational interests, and of course, girls. Donald continually struggled with the social expectations of teenage relationships, as many teens still do. The girls always wanted to dance!

Finishing high school in the 1930s, just as many jobs disappeared, left many young people despondent about their future prospects. By 1938, sixteen-year-old Donald was working in a low paying, unskilled job, facing a bleak outlook on life. While Donald was employed, thousands of other youths were not. For example, in the same year, two thousand "hungry, destitute, jobless youths from all parts of Canada staged a sit-down strike in Vancouver to bring attention to their opportunities and jobless future."[19] Yet many remained resilient.

In today's world, we are beginning to see a few attributes of Depression era struggles. It is not hard to find homeless people in tent cities, often with serious mental health and drug-related issues. During a global pandemic, our 2020 high school graduates were cut off from a celebration of their achievements and were left staring down the face of high unemployment and an uncertain future. Given that my generation has never confronted any extended economic depression, we would be wise to reflect upon the disparities of our society, and how we might tackle some of these problems in a sensible and meaningful manner.

Although we faced many challenges during the recent pandemic, we were also not confronted with a world war or the immediate prospect of one. By the late 1930s, a global conflict loomed large, and a war commenced in Europe. Teenagers of the time were criticized for both their new-found freedoms and their dependencies. Sound familiar? They were an easy target to be encouraged to prove their patriotism by enlisting. High school students were now wanted – young men for service overseas fighting the enemy, and young women to stabilize the home front. As the war began to pull many men away from their jobs and duties at home, women, especially young women, stepped in to provide their support. The road was long and continues to this day.

At the end of August 1939, the classic movie The Wizard of Oz was released to a national audience. Based on the children's fantasy novel The Wonderful Wizard of Oz by L. Frank Baum, the movie starred a young Judy Garland and told of her adventures to the land of Oz and back in a dream. The movie progressed from black and white to colour, featuring such memorable characters as the Munchkins, witches, scarecrows, a tin man, and a lion. The musical score featured timeless standards such as "Over the Rainbow" and "If I Only Had a Brain," and is widely considered to be the greatest movie of all time. The tale was a fantasy which captivated entire families.[20] The delightful film was about a young woman finding her way in a unique journey and adventurous manner. Realizing the importance of friends and family, the movie was a picture for the times.

Yet in a dark and very real sequel on September 1, 1939, German forces invaded Poland. A few days later, France and the United Kingdom declared war on Germany, and the Second World War began. A week later, Canada followed suit in declaring war on Germany. It seemed like a fantasy to many Canadian families, who huddled around their radios for updates while clouds of conflict languished overhead. The war progressed globally from 1939 to 1942 as Germany controlled most of the European nations and formed an alliance with Italy and Japan. By mid-1940, Germany occupied all of France, and the intensity of the war escalated with the bombing of Britain, war in the Balkans, and conflict across the Atlantic seas. In Canada, anxious families, many with strong, close family ties to Great Britain, followed daily newspaper reports and newsreels, and began to mourn the fallen soldiers daily. The emerging teenage culture was not about to end, but the nation's youth were soon confronted with a troubled country that desperately needed their service. The youngsters would not disappoint.

Footnotes Chapter 6

1 Cynthia Comacchio, *The Dominion of Youth: Adolescence and the Making of Modern Canada, 1920 to 1950* (Wilfrid Laurier University Press, 2008): 27.

2 Comacchio, *Dominion*, 27

3 Comacchio, *Dominion*, 26

4 Veronica Strong-Boar, "Janey Canuck: Women in Canada, 1919-1939", (Canadian Historical Association, 1994): 4.

5 E.S. Dummer, foreword, "The Unadjusted Girl, with Cases and Standpoint for Behavior Analysis", by W.I. Thomas (Boston, MA: Little, Brown, 1923), as quoted in Cynthia Comacchio, "The Dominion of Youth: Adolescence and the Making of Modern Canada, 1920 to 1950" (Wilfrid Laurier University Press, 2008): 27.

6 Comacchio, *Dominion*, 10, footnote 42.

7 DJM letter, March 3, 1943.

8 DJM letter, March 3, 1943.

9 DJM letter, March 3, 1943.

10 DJM letter, March 3, 1943.

11 Neil Sutherland, *Growing Up: Childhood in English Canada from the Great War to the Age of Television*, (University of Toronto Press, 1997): 139.

12 DJM letter, Dec 7, 1942.

13 *Kitchener Record*, Nov 26, 1943.

14 Jeff Hicks, "Old Kitchener Aud burned to the ground 70 years ago", *Waterloo Region Record*, January 8, 2018, https//2018/01/08/old-kitchener-aud-burned-to-the-ground-70-years-ago.html.

15 Along with thousands of other locals!

Footnotes cont'd

[16] Kevin Dupont, "For Bruins Legend Milt Schmidt, outdoor hockey was a rite of passage", *Boston Globe*, December 26, 2015, https://www.bostonglobe.com/sports/2015/12/26/bruins-legend-milt-schmidt-outdoor-hockey-was-rite-passage/6oZiKFsslCjhcAmkERpwcI/story.html.

[17] Dupont, "Bruins Legend."

[18] Somewhat ironically the same high school that I attended twenty-five years later.

[19] Arthur Woollacott, "Youth Salvage," *Macleans Magazine*, January 1, 1939, as cited in Comacchio, "The Dominion of Youth", 39.

[20] It remains to this day a family favourite and yes, I have seen the ruby slippers in person.

Chapter 7

The March to War

Then there was the war, and I married it because there was nothing else when I reached the age of falling in love.

- Guy Sajer

As the war took hold, the need for young men to join the effort became an imperative for the Canadian government. Politically, recruitment controversies had lingered after World War I, and the government wanted to avoid the same mistakes. Following the meetings on civilian recruitment, Lt. Col. James Mess, Director of Recruiting (Civilian), reported that "In World War I the Canadian infantry division had 4,400 horses and 153 motor vehicles …Today the infantry division has no horses, no wagons, but has 3,500 motor vehicles of 160 different types."[1] An industrial system supported by modern advances in manufacturing and engineering was a crucial element of the conflict. The growing demand for military personnel would be expanded, and the voluntary system of recruitment was pressed to "produce the goods" in terms of skilled and highly trained personnel. The reality on the ground was that an experienced and organized enemy fought using a new, grueling machinery of war.

The Canadian government of Mackenzie King wanted to avoid conscription. Accordingly, they substituted propaganda and coercion in attempts to enlist men, especially young men, for overseas duty. Recruiting efforts relied heavily on calling out youth for their patriotism. An editorial [2] published in the Toronto Globe and Mail on October 10, 1941, described a fellow in a military uniform stopping young men as they passed by on the street to interrogate them about their intentions to enlist. The young men were placed on the spot by the aggressive recruiter, "plainly chosen for that duty because of his quick and sharp wit and his not too courteous manner." The editorial was critical of the Prime Minister and his colleagues, who had garnered votes by pledging to never introduce conscription for overseas service. "Admittedly, this is everyone's war; so why not conscript manpower as well as wealth." They demanded that "all men of military age and qualifications go before, say, a board which could consider each case on its merits … the same treatment for all." The Globe's editorial argued for conscription, accusing the government of coercion, intimidation, and shaming naïve young men to do their patriotic duty while "others who are equally eligible remain untouched."

Young Donald, now eighteen years of age, was surely one of those naïve young men. He was poorly educated and an unskilled worker employed as a shoe treer in a factory. A sense of patriotism, duty to country, and a dose of coercion and intimidation led him and several of his friends, along with thousands of other teenagers, to enlist "voluntarily" for service overseas. In September 1941, just a few days before the Globe and Mail editorial was published, Donald tried to enlist in Hamilton, Ontario. He was not accepted into the service at that time; it could be he was too young, too inexperienced, or he walked away from completing his application. However, it was likely that Donald's education status – grade nine – was not suitable for his goal of air training. Many young men held the ideal of becoming an ace pilot but they seriously lacked the background. An education plan designed to bring the recruits up to standard for enlistment in air training was just beginning to be introduced in September of 1941. The following year an educational program was put in place, and Donald completed his enrollment at the recruitment centre in London, Ontario on September 5, 1942.

Near the conclusion of World War I the German forces had mounted aerial attacks on Great Britain. While the carnage of the Great War lay in the trenches across the channel, the flight of enemy aircraft over English townships prompted the creation of an independent arm of the military which could take to the skies and respond behind enemy lines. As the First World War ended, the role of aviation increased, and the establishment of an air force was imminent. Citing the prescient words of H.G. Wells that aviation would alter warfare forever, Dunmore and Carter in *Reap The Whirlwind* concluded "It would destroy an enemy's means of waging war by demolishing his factories. And, of even greater importance, it would wreck the morale of his people."[3]

Spurred by the lessons of World War I, the British Air Ministry's Bomber Command was expected to lead intense aerial attacks. However, as the air assaults made significant strides, so did enemy air defenses. By the time of the invasion of France, British aircrews "died by the score in desperate attacks .. as casualties mounted alarmingly."[4] Following little success in daytime air raids, and plagued by the inaccuracies of night raids, an area bombing strategy was adopted with the intent of destroying entire cities, industrial factories, and workers' morale. The campaign began in early 1942. As the air war escalated in the following months, the American allies arrived, and a newly formed Canadian Bomber squad, No. 6 RCAF Group, was put in place.

Canadian bomber squadrons were initially attached to the British Royal Air Force (RAF) groups. Then, a formation of the No. 6 Royal Canadian Air Force (RCAF) Group was advanced as an independent Canadian force and no longer merely a colonial servant. The Canadian Group comprised of eight squadrons, often under-strength and in need of everything from tools to experienced ground crews. As a result, the acceleration of the air war required an intensive training program to supply the force with the manpower needed to address the conflict.

The British Commonwealth Air Training Plan (BCATP) was originally created in agreement with the United Kingdom, Canada, Australia, and New Zealand to operate an aircrew training program. Since training in the United Kingdom was deemed to be too vulnerable to enemy attack, Canada was chosen as the location for the training facilities. The first BCATP-trained pilots had been posted to the British RAF by the end of 1941, but the introduction of Canada's No. 6 Bomber Group as an independent air force demanded a significant increase in the number of Canadians required to man the group. Additionally, "the segment of the population from which potential aircrew applicants could be drawn was becoming narrowly restricted."[5] In 1942, twenty-five percent of the recruits were under twenty years of age, and by 1943 that number rose to sixty per cent. The addition of younger recruits demanded more supplementary training, as many, like Donald, failed to meet the minimum educational standards required for aircrews. A significant cohort of young men needed to upgrade their current academic qualifications in order to meet Air Force standards.

Donald fit this mold. He was just a teenager when he enlisted on September 5, 1942, and on September 16 he reported to his first posting in Toronto for basic training. Two months later he was transferred to the Service Flying Training school at Burford, near Brantford, Ontario. While much time was spent learning new skills, there was still a measure of boring downtime for the young men to fill. In his foreword to *Rhyme and Reason*,[6] Col. Gilchrist suggests that if you give a soldier "a stub of lead pencil and a piece of paper … the first thing you know he's written a poem." Gilchrist wonders if all men are poets at heart given there is plenty of time to think in the army. He notes that soldiers routinely face "black, bleak nights when sleep does not come," giving them the time to self-reflect and scribble a few lines on the page. Donald was certainly not a poet, but as he made his way through basic training, boredom and loneliness marked his time and he wrote many letters. Donald often wrote his mom and sometimes his brother Carl, but especially his best friend Mel, from the time they joined the forces until the week before his death.

Unfortunately, Mel and Donald were never stationed in the same location. As a result, Donald was always trying to work out arrangements for them to get together, meet women, and for Donald to complain about his routine. In his letters, Donald never mentioned the features and politics of war, or the atrocities of the enemy. He focused on his loneliness and his desire to meet with Mel and his friends. At the training school, Donald complained that "I haven't even been to Brantford yet as it's too far from the station and the guys say there is nothing doing in town."[7] After his initial posting, Mel wrote to Donald to let him know that he was having a great time. Donald's experience was not the same. In his reply back to Mel on December 7, 1942, Donald writes, "Well I see you're happy in the service (and how) but you'll get used to it." Donald also complained that the only person who wrote to him was his mother, once a week, and occasionally his brother Carl.

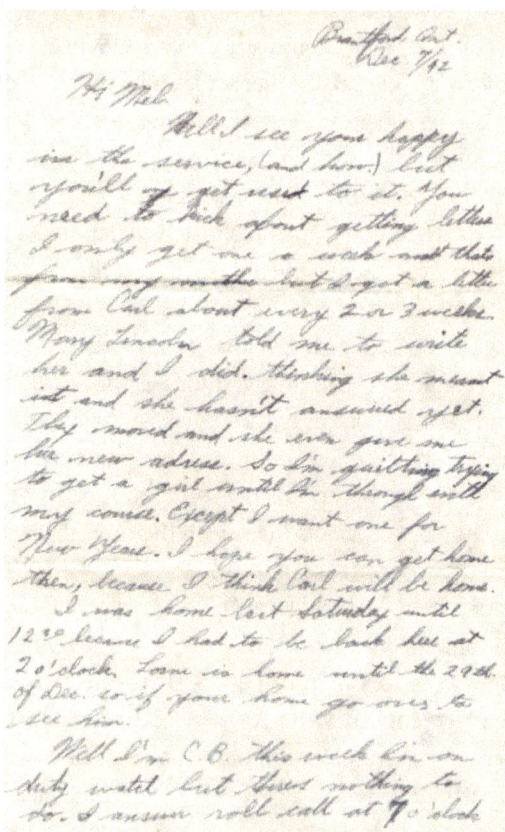

Donald's first letter, December 7, 1942

Women were always a topic of conversation between the two young men. While his buddy Mel was adept at dating, Donald struggled with establishing any kind of relationship with members of the opposite sex. It wasn't that he didn't try, as he told Mel "Mary Lincoln told me to write her and I did thinking she meant it ... she moved and even gave me her new address." However, he received no response and Donald announced to Mel that he "was quitting trying to get a girl," except of course – as Donald asserted in the very next sentence – that he wanted one on New Year's Eve!

As Gilchrist noted, soldiers find time in those "bleak, black nights" to write, and Donald was confined to barracks (C.B.) that week with little to do but write letters. Soldiers could be confined to barracks for many reasons, from being posted on duty to not wearing their beret properly. For Donald, alcohol and gambling often led him astray. He complained in his letter of leaving a card game down $2.50. Mel had similar experiences with gambling, and Donald, possibly by the encouragement of his mother, or having been disciplined, vowed to quit the pastime. He urged Mel to do the same, advising him to "not play on the next payday and save your money for Christmas and New Year's."

While Donald struggled with fostering relationships with the opposite sex, and wrestled with loneliness, not everything was hopeless in his training adventures. Donald enthusiastically told Mel that he finally "got what I've long been after – a plane ride!" He was in the air for two hours, taking sharp banks but sadly no loops. "It sure was nifty up there," he proclaimed, although he was quite cold because he wasn't wearing a flight suit. Donald's thrill with the sharp turns, and his naiveté that the plane might be taking loops, was often found in young men in the initial stages of their aircrew training as they tried to turn their ambitions into reality. They often dreamed of being a pilot and the next "Canadian Red Baron."[8] The BCATP was tasked to bring young aviators from an mindset of reckless abandon to one of proficiency and respect for their own well-being.

Matthew Chapman[9] described how problems with aerobatics and low flying resulted in numerous training crashes. By late 1941, aircrew trainees and their instructors experienced one hundred and seventy fatalities, with forty of them directly attributed to "low aerobatics and low flying."

The challenges the BCATP faced were widespread. Some of the instructors who were assigned to teach the courses also lacked any significant training in education. As a result most of the lessons were rote recitations of memorized military procedures, protocols, and academic curricula. It was certainly not an exciting undertaking for many of the young recruits like Donald, whose patriotism outmatched their enthusiasm (or lack of) for academic life and military rigour. As a result, the disciplinary measure for the young men was confinement to barracks (C.B.). Donald had his share of C.B. assignments, but dealt with them in his own way. In a postscript to Mel, he declared, "Just think I'm C.B. (confined to barracks) the night of my birthday but I'll be drunk." His loneliness seemed to spur his drinking, and he never once, in all of his correspondence with his buddy Mel, mentioned any other friends that he made during his service. Whenever he was given the opportunity for some leave, he came home to re-connect with Mel and his friends.

In a subsequent letter to Mel on January 10, 1943,[10] Donald, sitting around doing nothing, informed Mel that he was coming home the next weekend. Donald had written about another girl, Helen, who he was trying to meet when he was home. Much to Donald's chagrin, Mel could not make it home that weekend, and Donald set out alone to get together with some other friends and celebrate his leave. Donald wrote back to Mel about his weekend home: "What do you mean I must be having a lot of fun, I don't even know the meaning of the word anymore."[11] Donald had gone uptown and met a couple of hometown friends for a beer. Then they went skating at their favourite hangout, the beloved Granite Club, and stayed for the evening dance. The dancing always seemed to do Donald no favours, and he wrote no more about his hope of meeting up with Helen. She probably liked to dance!

Even though Donald struggled with meeting girls, it never stopped him from offering advice to Mel about his escapades with women. One time, Mel had met a prospective girlfriend in Listowel, and Donald – probably reflecting on his own despondency in relationships – advised his friend that he should hang on to her. And "don't get any funny ideas." Donald relayed to Mel that if there were any more women up in Listowel, he could make it up there some time. He also wanted to get home the following weekend for a party, and he was hoping that Mel could join him. The plan was to ask Donald's older brother Ivan to start buying beer the week before his leave began. Ivan, an avid drinker himself, was over twenty-one and could buy beer legally. However, because of rationing, you could only buy six pints of beer a day. If you wanted a party, you went every day for a week to buy beer and Ivan could always be counted on to pitch in for his younger brother. Hoping for some assistance on the female front, Donald requested Mel to ask his lady to "Bring her girlfriend down with her if she would like to come and she's my type (ahem), you know I could always use a girl." Donald's "ahem" displayed his wit and irony. His sarcasm was often self-deprecating as he wanted desperately to meet a girl, any girl. It was always on his mind; they just shouldn't like dancing.

Donald also informed Mel that several recruits who came to Brantford with him were being sent to McGill University, in Montreal, to continue their studies. Donald wanted to be assigned to that program, as his brother Carl was living and working in Montreal. Once again, his desire to be close to family or friends was paramount. On March 7, 1943, Donald received his wish and was transferred to Montreal to begin studies in the Pre-Air Crew Educational Detachment (PAED) at McGill University in Montreal. The RCAF had recognized that the junior matriculation educational standard required for aircrew training was reducing the number of potential recruits. Donald, with only a grade nine standing, was a good example of a recruit who needed to upgrade his education before advancing to aircrew training. Collaborating with universities across the country, the PAED program provided academic training in subjects such as mathematics, science, navigation, and English.

To proceed to the air gunner school, candidates had to obtain a mark of at least fifty percent or higher on all of their examinations. Donald did well in mathematics, achieving a grade of eighty-five, but he grumbled at learning grammar. To his dismay, the structure of a sentence – the subject, predicate, and verbs – held his mark to seventy-one. Nevertheless Donald appeared to do well when he applied himself, making me wonder why he would leave school after grade nine. I suppose I should relate well, having left school at seventeen; it's not always about your grades. On the military side, Donald did very well, achieving ninety-three percent in Aircraft Recognition and ninety-five percent in Signals.

At this time, Donald found himself on a university campus in a large, urban metropolis, and he continued to write to Mel, longing for home. The small-town boy in him protested that "this is a hell of a city, too big for me. Why you could put Toronto on one corner of it."[12] He noted that the snow in the city was melting, and they were still skiing up on the hill.

Skiing and skating were always on his mind, as Donald

reunited with his brother Carl; they attended a Montreal Canadiens hockey game on Saturday, March 13, 1943, versus the Chicago Blackhawks. Carl was working in Montreal for RCA Victor and had come to know a fellow at work who was a security guard at the hockey games. Carl could slip his colleague a "buck", and he and a couple of friends would sneak in the back door. On this night, Donald was treated to a six-six tie in an exciting match by two teams who were competing to make the playoffs. The next week the Canadiens played the Boston Bruins in the playoffs.

Unfortunately, Donald's treasured hometown hockey heroes, Schmidt, Durant, and Bauer, had already left the team to join the forces. Donald's brother Carl recounted how he had seen the Ottawa RCAF Flyers play an exhibition game with Schmidt, Durant, and Bauer in the lineup. Carl, who knew Schmidt's wife Marie from Kitchener, waited to see them in the foyer after the game. However, Carl laughed as he recalled how Milt and Marie were kissing and hugging, so he left them alone. Even though Carl could say hello to Marie, Milt was too big a star to inconvenience. Donald would continue to keep tabs on his idol, Milt Schmidt, who would eventually be stationed near him in England. Little did Donald know that, as he watched his favourite activity, he was spending his last few hours with his brother Carl. Carl never forgot.

In a strange twist of fate, an event was taking place overseas on that very day which could have changed the course of Donald's service dramatically. On March 13, 1943, Hitler was handed a parcel bomb, that he thought was a gift for two of his officers, as he boarded a plane. The conspirators in Berlin were ready to assume control of the government on Hitler's death. The plane took off, but a defective detonator failed to ignite the bomb[13] and Hitler survived to lead the Nazi insurgence, and innumerable young men like Donald, to their ultimate demise.

The next day, Carl and Donald went to visit "The Kids." The Kids, were better known to everyone as "The Harmony Kids," and featured siblings Robert, Lloyd, Kay, and Joyce Hahn, who played professionally as a popular musical quartet. Their parents, Harvey and Mary, were cousins to Donald's family. The Harmony Kids made their way from Saskatchewan all the way to New York, one time appearing on the popular radio network show "We the People."[14] When the war started, Lloyd and Bob were eligible for the draft and preferred to serve in the Canadian Forces, so the entire family moved to Montreal. Lloyd, like Donald, entered training as an air gunner and was eventually shot down over the North Sea and taken prisoner of war. He lost one arm in his ordeal but returned to Canada after the war, where he and Donald's brother Carl started a lasting friendship. Donald wrote to Mel that they sat around and talked, then Carl, Kay, and he went to a show.

Donald also wrote to his mother that they went out to a night club and had a "ginger ale" (ahem!). He sent the receipt for the drinks so his mom could see how expensive it was living in Montreal. Kay's younger sister Joyce, then a tiny fourteen-year-old, had to stay home. One can imagine how Donald would have reacted a decade later when Joyce Hahn became Canada's sweetheart, hosting the Cross Country Hit Parade with Wally Koster and hitting the national charts in the United States with her hit song "Gonna Find Me a Bluebird."[15] Maybe he would have been inspired to learn how to dance!

In Montreal, Donald was able to connect with some family members and a few friends. Always the small-town boy, life in the metropolis remained a daily ordeal for him. "The only good thing about Montreal is the shows on Sundays and you can get it when you want it".

"The shows cost sixty-two cents a ticket and the other has different prices," he said. A popular hangout for young men at this time was the Gayety Theatre, where Donald and his brother would stop by for some "entertainment." The Gayety was known for such antics as "weird and wonderful routines involving bath tubs, giant parrots, Buddhist temples and chastity belts." [16] In other words, a strip club. The "other" was prostitution. Donald didn't elaborate in his letters about the ladies of the evening; he told Mel he would tell him about it when he saw him. Garnet Robertson [17] was another young recruit who followed the same training program as Donald. On his stay in Montreal, he wrote:

One of the guys on the course and I each had a dollar and he wanted to go to the house of prostitution. We matched to see who got the two dollars – and he won. We asked a policeman the directions and he showed us. Once there we were taken to a room where six fat and forty women in kimonos were lined up. He told them that he only had two dollars, so they showed us the door very quickly. That was one day I was glad that I was broke."

If you were in the military the police had your back, but for Donald, even spending a few dollars was not an easy task. Always the cheapskate, Donald went out for supper with a friend and he cried, "it cost $1.62!" He continually moaned, "The cost of living sure is high down here." One day Donald went for a haircut and "the guy put on a little shampoo" and it cost him $1.65 – "I almost took a flip when he said that." Maybe it was a Depression era apprehension about money, or a lack of resources that kept Donald aware of the cost of living, or maybe it was his feeling that any money spent on a haircut and a meal was not available for beer and gambling.

Connecting with girls, whether in Montreal, at home, or just through his letter writing, remained a tall task for Donald. He constantly wrote the ladies back home letters, and it always seemed that after a brief correspondence they no longer wanted to write back to him. "Well Mel I'm without a girl again, I've written Mary twice and she hasn't replied yet so that's that."[18] Donald mourned that he only had Mel and his mother to write to, and his loneliness was evident. For Donald, Montreal was unfriendly and expensive, too large for his liking, and there were those darn girls.

In one special moment, he bragged to Mel that he was attending school at the university and on his recent math test, likely an initial assessment, he scored 100 percent! Donald had successfully completed his upgrading and was transferred on April 3, 1943 to No. 1 Air Gunners Ground Training School (A.G.G.T.S.), Quebec City. A newly established training facility, No. 1 A.G.G.T.S. opened in March 1943 because of a critical shortage of aerial gunners overseas. The six-week program at the school included some physical training and the use, care and maintenance of small arms and machine guns used on aircraft.

Donald was mostly bored in Quebec City, but he was not a lone wolf in his feelings about the location. Garnet Robertson also wrote of his experiences in the Quebec facility. The facility was an old orphanage, six stories high, which had been condemned. He called the mess hall "just that, a mess." "The grub was terrible and the flies were so thick you could hardly walk through them." Even though the facility was in poor condition, training continued. Donald wrote to Mel, who was now stationed in Ipperwash, Ontario, that he could take a Vickers machine gun apart and put it back together again. Also learning how to handle pistols and rifles, Donald scoffed that "when I leave here, I'll be shooting everything but a cannon."

Even though he had only one week left in his training program in Quebec City, Donald did not know whether he was going to be sent to Toronto or Mt. Joli. By this time, it didn't matter; nothing was going well in Quebec City, and he wrote Mel despairingly that "I hope you can make out this writing, but I'm drunk as an old fart. I get drunk every night now. I'm fed up with this joint and don't give a shit anymore. The French language is getting on my nerves." He still longed to meet a girl but bitterly complained, "It's a bitch down here, you can't find any women who speak English." Meeting a young woman companion in Quebec City was not going to happen, so Donald continued his writing, sending more letters to Betty and another girl, Verna. He decided he was finished with Mary. "I wish I knew what I did to make her stop writing," he wondered. While Donald asked Mel to check why Mary stopped writing, he said, "don't give her shit, I don't want her to write if she has to be coaxed."

In our teenage years, relationships are mostly about having fun, discovering ourselves, and fitting in with others. We bolster our self-esteem when we are accepted, and ache when we are rejected. Often our reactions are spontaneous, and we step in when we should step back, and step back when we should step in. Donald had a way of stepping up to offer his friend Mel advice as his wingman, albeit breaking most wingman rules, but he struggled with an awareness of his own endeavours. A female friend of Mel's, Betty, had written Donald that she really liked Mel but that he wasn't bothering with her. Putting his foot in his mouth, Donald wrote a letter to tell her that Mel was seeing another woman named Rose. Maybe Donald was trying to catch one of the girls on the rebound from Mel by consoling her. He told Mel, "I thought I better tell Betty because she was falling too hard for you." Donald was hoping that Mel wasn't too angry with him, but let him know that if he wanted to make up with Betty, "just blame it on me." Donald always wanted to keep his best friend by his side.

After completing his six-week training course in Quebec City, Donald was transferred to the Bombing and Gunnery unit at Mont Joli, Quebec, on May 16, 1943. Mont Joli was 300 km northeast of Quebec City, on the south shore of the St. Lawrence River in the Gaspe region of Quebec. It had a regional airport but was pretty much located in the middle of nowhere. Preparation picked up at Mont Joli and the boys were kept busy; things were starting to get serious now. The normal routine would be up at 6:00 am, breakfast, train until noon, lunch, and more training at 1:00 pm. Robertson described the air gunners' routine flying Fairey Battles:[19]

Gunners would go up two at a time. One gunner in the turret and one sitting on the floor near the engine cooler. You would get the fumes from the engine and would usually come down feeling lousy. One plane would fly along with us towin' a 'drough' (drogue) which was a canvas affair something like a parachute. We shot so many rounds at it and they would count the holes when we landed to see how we had done.[20]

At 5:00 pm there was physical training, then supper at 6:00 pm. After supper, cards and studying. Donald struggled with the program; he was sick some days, yet he had to train until 9:30 pm. He confessed to Mel, "I'm all fucked out already and I don't know how I'll last for five more weeks." As he waded through his despair, he managed to continue to mark his achievements. Donald received a promotion from Leading Air

Craftsman (L.A.C.) to Air Craftsman Second Class (A.C.2) and looked forward to the rank of sergeant, which he hoped to achieve in another four weeks. Mel was thinking of coming to Mt. Joli to visit Donald – perhaps because, from his previous letter, he knew his best friend was not doing very well – but Donald discouraged him because of the lack of train connections. However, Donald still aimed to be the mediator in Mel's love life, receiving another letter from Betty about how much she loved Mel (who was still seeing Rose). Donald wasn't coming home though, and he finished by saying, "I'll be seeing you over there." The boys, with many other young Canadians, would soon be on their way across the Atlantic to join the war effort.

On June 25, 1943, Donald completed his training and received his Air Gunners' badge and new rank of sergeant. By this time, air crews were being lost overseas on a regular basis and new recruits were needed to fill the vacancies. The next stop was Halifax, where he would board a ship to transport the airmen abroad for service to his country. And hopefully it would give Donald a chance to connect with his best friend Mel, enjoy a beer or two, and maybe even meet some girls. That is, if they didn't dance.

Footnotes Chapter 7

[1] James Mess, "The Gentleman in Battledress." (Ottawa: Department of National Defense, 1941):.45

[2] Editorial, "Coercion by Subterfuge," *The Globe and Mail*, Oct 10, 1941: 6.

[3] Spencer Dunmore, and William Carter, *Reap the Whirlwind, The Untold Story of 6 Group, Canada's Bomber Force of World War II*, (McClelland & Stewart, 1991): 3.

Footnotes cont'd

⁴ Dunmore, *Reap the Whirlwind*, 5.

⁵ F.J. Hatch, *Aerodrome of Democracy: Canada and the British Commonwealth Air Training Plan 1939-1945*, (Canadian Government Publishing Centre, Ottawa, 1983): 179.

⁶ C.W. Gilchrist, *Rhyme and Reason: A Souvenir Volume of Verse by Canadian Soldier-Poets,* (Canadian Public Relations Services, Rome, Italy, 1945).

⁷ DJM letter, Dec 7, 1942.

⁸ Matthew Chapman, "BCATP revisited. The Wartime Evolution of Flight Training in Canada", *Canadian Air Force Journal*, 5, No. 2, (Spring 2011): 14.

⁹ Chapman, "BCATP," p.11.

¹⁰ This date is ironically my birthdate (I was born ten years later).

¹¹ DJM letters, March 3, 1943.

¹² DJM letters, March 16, 1943.

¹³ A&E Television Networks, "Another Plot To Kill Hitler Foiled", http://www.history.com/this-day-in-history/another-plot-to-kill-hitler-foiled.

¹⁴ Martin Melhuish, "The Hahn Family's Remarkable Canadian Music Legacy". (Music Publishers Canada, 2016), https://www.musicpublisher.ca/2091-2.

¹⁵ Joyce Hahn, YouTube video, https://www.youtube.com/watch?v=JinlubbgtvQ

¹⁶ Jim Burke, "Last Night at the Gayety: A musical ode to Montreal's Sin City era when striptease star Lili St. Cyr reigned supreme." *Montreal Gazette*, April 21, 2016, https://montrealgazette.com/entertainment/last-night-at-the-gayety-a-musical-ode-to-montreals-sin-city-era-when-striptease-star-lili-st-cyr-reigned-supreme.

Footnotes cont'd

[17] Garnet Robertson, "Ghost Squadron." Commonwealth Air Training Plan Museum, https://bcatp.org/109-garnet-robertson-oh.

[18] DJM letters, April 16, 1943.

[19] The Fairey Battle was a British bomber used by the RAF at the beginning of the war. The plane was slow and subject to many losses. By the end of 1940 it was removed from service and used by aircrew training centers.

[20] Robertson, "Ghost Squadron."

Chapter 8

England

The news from home, those precious lines, From loved ones many miles away, Instils our weary, tattered minds, With courage for another day.

– G. H. Adlam[1]

The No. 1 "Y" Depot in Halifax, Nova Scotia, was a boarding port for all Air Force personnel heading overseas to the United Kingdom. While some men could remain in Halifax for up to a month, Donald arrived on July 9, 1943, and was able to board his ship one week later. Other than a morning parade and roll call, the airmen did not have much to keep themselves occupied while they waited anxiously to depart. The boys worried about German U-boats prowling the north Atlantic; some had even entered the Gulf of St. Lawrence, at times nearing the training center at Mont Joli. However, for the most part, troop ships sailed in convoys and were well protected. Once on board your vessel, the ocean crossing took six days, with little to do as the ship tossed about the ocean blue. Vern White,[2] a young air bomber in training who flew out of the same base as Donald, described his crossing from No. 1 "Y" Depot:

I remember looking out of a porthole one day to see a smaller ship tossing and pitching in the angry sea. The bow would completely disappear with the stern rising out of the water and its propeller churning in mid-air before settling back in the water. This process was repeated again and again and went on for several days.

Lifeboat drills took place daily, but most of the time, if they did not have weak stomachs, the men took to playing cards. Card games were a pastime Donald always enjoyed, especially since there was no need for him to save his money. White, on his voyage, observed:

Another recollection I have is the poker games that seem to go on all night. When the guys tired of poker they switched to craps. There were a few big winners but mostly losers."[3]

There was no bragging by Donald or cheques sent home to his mother from winning at cards, so Donald resided in the "mostly losers" crowd. Navigating the seas seemed to be the easy part as the young men, bored with inactivity, reflected on their lives, friends, family, and wondered if they were ever coming home.

The RCAF aircrews arriving in the United Kingdom were initially assigned to the No. 3 Personnel Reception Centre (PRC) in Bournemouth. Here they waited for relocation to an Overseas Training Unit (OTU). Bournemouth is a seaside resort on the south coast of Great Britain, just across the channel from Le Havre, France. Aircrew members were typically housed in the local hotels and had to stay in the resort area for as long as four months, until a posting became available.

The area, popular with British holiday goers, sounded like an ideal setting to welcome weary Allied soldiers to their new assignments. Donald and his fellow recruits anxiously looked forward to their layover. After all, they survived the morbid conditions in Quebec City, the training regime in Mont Joli, and a jaded ocean crossing. Let the fun begin! Beach time! Women! Maybe even some who did not want to dance!

Donald, along with another Kitchener native son, Alex McEwan, was photographed as their ship arrived in England, and the photo appeared in the newspaper.[4] Their faces, stoic and lacking enthusiasm, must have been tempered by the realities of a wartime blackout and limited exposure to new and exciting experiences a young man could dream about on their arrival.

ARRIVE IN BRITAIN—Sgt. Don Metz, left, and Sgt. Alex McEwan, both of Kitchener, get their first glimpse of the British Isles just before disembarking from the troopship which safely carried them and hundreds of other R.C.A.F. air crew across the Atlantic.

Robert Collins was a prairie boy who had followed a similar path as Donald from the Mont Joli training base to England. Even though the accommodations at their new home were dubious, Collins considered his life a step up from Mont Joli:

> *We detrained at Bournemouth on the south coast, to be billeted in hotels of faded elegance. They had no staffs or services — just damp, chilly, barren rooms with beds, communal toilets, and crumbling plaster — but were infinitely more romantic than Mont Joli.*[5]

For Donald and many other new airmen, leaving behind Mont Joli was their great escape. At Bournemouth, the anticipation for their final aircrew training began to build for every new cast of young men destined for service. Collins recorded in his *Ordinary Airmen's War* that "Here fresh supplies of pilots, navigators, bomb aimers, wireless operators, and air gunners were literally stockpiled until needed."[6] Still, the young men were often held back. Doug Harvey, an aviator with the 408 Squadron, also followed a similar path as Donald from Bournemouth on to Leeming in Yorkshire. He described in *Boys, Bombs and Brussels Sprouts*, the airmen waiting in Bournemouth being "locked in a town that catered to retirees,"[7] with the boys bored, tired of make-work schedules, and yearning for an aircraft.

Unfortunately, the east coastal location was also an easy target for German Luftwaffe raids. German air raids on the town of Bournemouth were not uncommon, but the most devastating raid took place on May 23, 1943. The Allied Forces had just executed the infamous Dam Busters raid, which triggered catastrophic flooding in the Ruhr Valley in Germany, killing thousands in the local population. The Nazis, planning their revenge, surmised that if they destroyed planes, more planes would easily be at the ready. But, if they killed airmen their replacements would take a prolonged time to train. Thus, the Germans targeted the aircrews stationed at Bournemouth in retaliation.

Nick Churchill recounted how that day began:

That spring Sunday was bright and sunny, much like any other. By lunchtime the town centre streets and gardens of Bournemouth were teeming and the hotel dining rooms were filling up with people about to sit down to Sunday roast. In suburban back gardens across the conurbation, young children played as they waited for their mothers to call them in for dinner.[8]

It seemed like a normal day. But the serenity of the beachside resort quickly transformed as German fighters flew across the English Channel at sea level to avoid radar, and bombed the center of town. In a matter of minutes, twenty-two buildings were destroyed and more than three thousand others sustained damage. In this Bournemouth raid, "hundreds of Canadian airmen were staying at the Metropole Hotel, and the Central Hotel was similarly full of Australians." Almost 200 service members died that day. "In little more than a minute … Bournemouth fell victim to its bloodiest raid of World War II." Hotels, a children's orphanage, a church, department stores, parks, roads, and homes were bombed or strafed, devastating the seaside resort. The Bournemouth Municipal Orchestra was scheduled to play a concert broadcast by the BBC that day. Refusing to give the Germans a propaganda victory they played on, in tribute to those who died that day.

Donald and a new convoy of recruits from Halifax arrived at Bournemouth on July 23, 1943, exactly two months after the infamous Bournemouth raid. They arrived to a devastated town. There was nothing pleasant about staying in the community at this time. The town stayed calm and carried on while the aircrew members adjusted to their new boredom. Their homesickness alternated with their anxiety as they waited in anticipation of joining the fray. The men lived in fear of further attacks, with little or nothing to do but bunker down, turn the lights off, clean up, and wait for their re-assignment.

Donald stayed for a month in Bournemouth before being transferred to the No. 22 Operational Training Unit (22 OTU). OTUs of the RAF were the training units that prepared aircrews on a specific aircraft. The 22 OTU was situated nearby the town of Wellesbourne, Mountford as a division of the Canadian No. 6 RCAF Group. The Wellesbourne airfield was situated only a few kilometers from the Stratford-upon-Avon theatre. If the recruits had wandered over to take in a play, they might have heard an angry Mowbray, the Duke of Norfolk in Shakespeare's Henry IV, hail "we're ready to fight to the last man." Indeed, the boys could now stand alongside Lord Hastings when he replied, "And if those of us who are here should fail, we have reinforcements standing by." The Canadian boys had arrived, and they stood ready to take the place of the fallen.

Donald continued to write to his buddy Mel to let him know where he was stationed, as both were in a period of transferring to different bases. Mel, who was now located with the No. 1 Royal Canadian Ordnance Corps (CORU), had connected with another mutual friend from home, Ted. It was August 20 and Donald was hoping the three of them could get together for "some piss poor beer." He had received mail from home from a girl who wanted Mel to write to her. Donald remained the loyal wingman for the heartbreaker Mel, passing on the information and wondering, "Does Ted know any women down here?"

Douglas Harvey, a young twenty-year-old pilot in the summer of 1943, wrote of his experience meeting and courting the single English ladies. He noted that "most of the eighteen- and nineteen-year-old Canadian kids who went to war were incredibly naïve." Describing his buddies' escapades of meeting and making out with the local girls, Harvey concluded that the "English girls must have thought a flock of eunuchs had landed in their midst."[9] Nevertheless, he felt the English lasses were delighted to meet them. Much to Donald's chagrin, it turned out they also loved dancing.

Donald wrote to Mel again on September 1,[10] after finally receiving two letters from him. Apparently, Mel was eating well, which prompted Donald to complain about his meals and how he had to pay a three-pence mess fee. He was now finishing his training and hoping to move up to a Canadian Squadron. The training typically included cross-country flights, night flying, and simulated bombing runs. Donald wrote that he had three more nighttime cross-country trips to complete before he would be moved to his next stage of training. After his last flight, he hoped to get a leave to meet up with Mel and Ted.

On the 9th of September, Donald was moved to the 1659 Conversion Unit (CU) at Topcliffe, Yorkshire, and following a leave, he was transferred to the 1664 CU training unit. On his leave, Donald had a difficult time finding his friend Mel, and his frustration was evident. In his letter written on September 13 and mailed from Aldershot, he barked at Mel, "Why the hell don't you let me know where you are!"

Donald had travelled down from the village of Topcliffe in Yorkshire, to Aldershot to try to connect with his friends. By train, the journey would likely take the full day, at least an uncomfortable eight-hour ride, but Donald desperately wanted to see his pals. He tried to find their mutual friend Ted, with no luck, and then headed to where he thought Mel was stationed, near the town of Brighton, another few hours away on the English Channel coast. Angry he couldn't find his buddies, he complained that he "can't get in the fucking joint." Donald returned to Aldershot where he wrote Mel to say he had received a letter from Mel's brother Wilf, but Wilf did not tell him where he was stationed, either. "I'm sitting here all alone, I guess I'll go back in a day or two ... this is the worst leave I've ever spent." Despite his frustration, Donald finished his letter with "Hope to see you next leave."

Donald was then moved to the 1664 CU in Croft, near Darlington. He wanted to find Mel and wrote him on October 1, wondering, "What the hell, is it a military secret where you are or what?" He expected to stay at the Croft field for only three weeks, as his crew was beginning to take shape. At the 1664 CU, Donald's training began on the Handley Page Halifax aircraft, and his crew was established. Spencer Dunmore suggested that when you are assigned to your crew it was when the boys stopped thinking of themselves as individuals and became part of a team. One might think that the crews were assigned according to a precise set of criteria; however, the crewing process was often left up to the airmen themselves.

It was as simple as ushering groups of pilots, navigators, bomb aimers, wireless operators, and air gunners into a large room, often a hangar, and telling them to "get on with it." [11]

Barney Rawson, who was the acting 429 Squadron Leader in Leeming and a very talented young pilot, recalled his selection to an aircrew almost a year earlier. As Rawson put it, "we crewed together, green as grass"[12] at 22 OTU. Like kids in the school yard, some crews were formed simply because they were the last ones standing in the selection process. Others had to be assigned depending on the need and availability for certain positions. In any event, the crews bonded quickly, as they were about to enter a fearsome conflict together, depending on one another for success and survival. They were now a "sprog" unit, as the freshmen crews were called, and posted to 429 Squadron together on October 27, 1943. The 429 Squadron, known as the Bison squadron, sported the motto "Fortunae nihil" – nothing to chance – and their training base was in Leeming, Yorkshire.

Final training preparations could be as challenging and dangerous as the regular operations. Sprog units experienced fatal training accidents at an alarming rate. Although the BCATP program was considered a favourable part of the Canadian military education experience, it had a circuitous route to success. The system had evolved from its pre-war, "stick and rudder" skills training for bush pilots to a sophisticated training regimen on instrument flying procedures. Modern warfare now involved "highly sophisticated, multi-system, high performance aircraft in increasingly adverse atmospheric conditions."[13]

In a letter to Mel on October 13, Donald told him that on the night he wrote from Wellesborne on September 1, he was involved in a training crash, but he was not hurt. Fatal accidents at OTUs were not uncommon, for a variety of reasons. One controversial assessment suggested that the aircrews were sub-standard in their training, especially with respect to navigating in poor weather, nighttime, and blackout settings.[14] A main component of British weather at this time of year was a hazy fog, reducing the visibility of the horizon, making nighttime flying extremely risky.

In the two and a half years of 6 Group's war, scores of smashed aircraft would litter the craggy hills, the victims of mist or smoke, inaccurate navigation, sometime mechanical failure and battle damage, but more often, a fatal lack of experience."[15]

The continuous loss of RCAF aircrew members in the bombing campaigns demanded new replacement crews over ever shorter periods of time. Donald's crew of seven airmen now began their final preparation to fly the Handley Page Halifax on a bombing mission. A Halifax aircrew was made up of seven members who worked together as a team to achieve the goal of reaching their target, dropping their payload, and returning home safely.

Donald wrote again to Mel on October 31st that he was now situated at Leeming, Yorkshire, with the 429 Squadron, nicknamed the Bison Squadron. The members of his aircrew included pilot Willys Bloch from Vancouver; navigator Don Hogg from Thamesford, Ontario; Earl Burton, an air bomber from Zealandia, Saskatchewan; and Peter McCallum, an air gunner from Winnipeg, Manitoba. They were joined by two British RAF members: wireless operator Victor McGray and flight engineer Timothy Wainwright.

Will Bloch was the designated team leader and commanded the operations. Despite the criticism of BCATP's training of pilots, Bloch had received an evaluation of "a pilot of above average ability both by day and by night, who should make a reliable captain."[16] Hogg had the job of navigator. He was to keep the aircraft on course to arrive at the target area, and following the raid, get them home. The undertaking is much more difficult than it seems when you are flying in a stream of bombers, which could number in the hundreds. Harsh weather and poor visibility often led navigators off course, and being chased by a German night fighter on the return trip was always a challenging possibility.

Wainwright, an avid rugby enthusiast from Southport, UK, managed all the mechanical, hydraulic, electrical, and fuel systems, and served as the pilot's first assistant in take-off and landing. Burton, the air bomber, guided the aircraft during its bombing run. He had to remain prone in the front of the airplane and shout directions for the bombs to be released. The air bomber also served as the team's reserve pilot. McGray, another RAF recruit, served as the wireless operator who would record, send and receive all messages transmitted between the aircraft and the base, in addition to assisting the navigator. Finally, McCallum and Metz were the air gunners who would defend the plane against enemy attacks. They would warn the pilot of enemy air maneuvers for evasive actions to take place.

The air gunners, isolated from the rest of the crew in the mid and rear turrets, managed their positions alone.

The aircrew continued their training, sometimes as a team and at other times within their own specialties. They attended lectures on night flying, sea rescues and security, and flew cross-country training runs with air-to-air firing. They practiced safety procedures in case of a crash landing, like parachuting and strategies for exiting the plane. The air gunners also practiced skeet shooting and how to manage and manipulate air turrets. Other crew members studied the GEE navigation system, and pilots put time in on the link trainers, practicing how to fly by instruments. Some crews would occasionally do sea searches for airmen who had bailed from their flight over water. If they located a dinghy, they would relay the location to a rescue unit.

All crew members practiced dinghy survival skills, and one of the instructors in northeastern England at this time was none other than Donald's hometown hockey hero, Milt Schmidt. There is a somewhat surprising parallel between Donald's and Milt's experiences overseas. Milt had attended Bombing and Gunnery school like Donald, and was similarly posted overseas to the No. 6 Group of the Royal Canadian Air Force, which was part of the Bomber Command. While the members of hockey's famous Kraut line (Schmidt, Dumart, and Bauer) spent much of their service playing for morale-boosting Air Force hockey teams, Schmidt also served as a physical education instructor. He was posted to northeastern England in the same region as his super fan Donald, where he "conducted training sessions in a swimming pool as he taught airmen the tricky maneuvers in which a raft is inflated and flipped."[17]

Hockey was integral to the Canadian way of life, especially for young men, and Donald was no exception. To maintain morale and help stave off the insufferable boredom of waiting between missions, a 12-team RCAF league was established, and tournaments were held on bases and in English townships in the region. At one time, Dumart's team, located at the RCAF Station Linton-on-Ouse, beat Schmidt's team, based at the RCAF Middleton St. George, for the league championship.

Both locations were a mere thirty minutes away from Donald's post in Leeming, and Donald followed their exploits. Donald, still carrying his ice skates in his kit bag, wrote to Mel to let him know when Milt was promoted to P.O. (Pilot Officer). A Pilot Officer was not necessarily a pilot; the designation was more of a position title as opposed to a rank. However, it was now required to call Milt "Sir." I am sure that designation was not an issue to his devotee, Donald. Perhaps it was a dream of Donald's, after all these years and with his skates still in his bag, to share the same ice with Milt again, not as an ice scraper but as a hockey line mate.

Besides watching hockey and participating in the usual station parades, training, inspections, and occasional exams, Donald had a few other opportunities to occupy his time. For entertainment, the airmen could attend regular film nights and a variety of concerts with dance music often provided by the RAF White Wings orchestra. I doubt Donald made any great strides on the dance floor, but undoubtedly he enjoyed some of the movies. Perhaps *The Pride of the Yankees*, about baseball's late Lou Gehrig, caught his sports eye, or maybe the gambling, intrigue, and wartime story of the infamous *Casablanca* would furnish a few moments of entertainment in contrast to the often-boring ritual of training.

Sometimes additional special events were planned to help improve the airmen's morale. On one occasion at Leeming, the 427 Squadron was "adopted" by the movie studio Metro-Goldwyn-Mayer.[18] Each of their aircraft was named after an MGM star. Since the most popular choice for every aircrew was the lovely Lana Turner, a draw was held to determine which crew's plane would be adorned with the likes of the popular blonde beauty. But other than special events, the most favoured pastime for the men was the local watering holes in the nearby village of Bedale. After Donald's experience in Quebec with the accent of the French-speaking ladies, I am sure the thick British dialect of the young Bedale ladies was also a substantial mission to circumnavigate.

The new aircrew became a committed team. Donald, who regularly tried to find and meet his best friend Mel, formed a resilient allegiance with his squad members. Although he spent many lonely hours writing and searching for his friend, the crew at this time became a central part of his life. Training with his crew, Donald wrote to Mel that "if you move let me know and when I get leave, I'll be coming down there." However, he set an additional condition "that is if all the crew don't go out together." The men were well aware that not everybody always returned from a bombing mission, and they would survive or perish together. They were a team, and like most teams, they proudly displayed their allegiance in the mandatory "team photo," with the aircrew[19] in full dress in front of their plane.

Donald's aircrew was getting close to their first assignment. Before a crew could head out on their first mission, the pilot would go on one or more "second dickey" trips. The second dickey was a co-pilot who flew with a seasoned pilot to get acquainted with how an experienced crew performed in real-life operations. Bloch's initial second dickey outing was on the November 3, 1943 raid on Dusseldorf, as part of an aircraft raid from the 3, 4, 6, and 9 Groups that mounted three hundred and ninety planes in the attack. On this mission, the squadrons experienced just a few clouds, and the visibility was good. Still, a total of twenty-three planes were lost in the raid. Twenty-five crews from the 6 Group had joined the attack and of these, two crews were lost and did not return home. Although Bloch's plane encountered no resistance, one other 429 Squadron plane was attacked by a night fighter and returned fire, performing a corkscrew maneuver to avoid the night fighter, who ultimately disengaged.

Bloch's final second dickey ride was in the November 18 raid on Mannheim, joining an airstream of five hundred and eighty-nine planes. On this raid, most crews struggled with their navigational aids and many missed their targets, including Bloch's dickey crew who had to jettison their bombs. The entire raid concluded with mixed results: several of the planes experienced icing, visibility varied, and a number of aircraft bombed Frankfurt as opposed to Mannheim. Sixteen aircraft from the 429 Squadron participated, and one plane was shot down by a night fighter and did not return.

The airmen dealt with these types of tragic losses on a regular basis. Bombing raids could involve as many as 1,000 planes, and on every mission, at least some aircraft never returned to their home base. Plane losses of five percent were considered good as they faced a variety of risks throughout the mission. Some planes would crash on the runway at takeoff, others experienced mechanical problems and turned back, and still others were victims of German defenses. Some planes even collided in midair accidentally within their own cohort. Even if a crew survived the bombing raid and evaded German night fighters, poor airstrips and weather conditions made crash landings common. Following each raid, the aircrew learned that some of their colleagues were declared dead, missing, wounded, or had become prisoners of war. Every squadron went through joyful periods when all returned safely, and experienced periods of adversity when multiple crews were lost. One day you could be sitting in the pub sharing a beer with a mate, celebrating a successful run, and the next day you could be found in the chapel, praying for his soul.

The No. 6 Group completed over 40,000 raids during the war. A total of 814 aircraft and approximately 5,700 airmen did not return from operations, and 4,203 airmen lost their lives.[20] At the end of the war, the airmen who returned home often continued to suffer the physical and mental wounds brought on as the result of their duties. Barney Rawson,[21] a member of the 429 Squadron at this time, exemplified the pressures of the job at hand for young men. Rawson was born in Smooth Rock Falls in northern Ontario the exact same week as Donald in 1922, and he was an exemplary member of the RCAF, becoming the youngest wing commander in the RCAF at the age of twenty-one. Rawson was given the Distinguished Flying Cross (DFC) in October 1943, just as Donald arrived at the Leeming base.

Barney Rawson was, without doubt, a talented young aviator who everyone looked up to with admiration. He had completed over fifty missions, covering an array of operations that not all aircrew members would expect to achieve during their service. His Bomber Command duties included the more routine sea searches and "gardening" (gardening was the laying of mines in enemy waters), as well as the more hazardous missions such as the bombing of industrial cities on German soil. Barney was also an articulate writer, even at a young age, and he often wrote long letters home to his friends and family. He also organized a squadron newsletter making numerous contributions about 429's activities and accomplishments.

Rawson's citation for the DFC said, "he has at all times set a fine example of courage, enthusiasm and devotion to duty." On the day following Donald's first mission, Rawson was appointed the group's tactic officer. He served for the duration of the war before returning home in 1945 to take up law studies at Osgoode Hall in Toronto. He continued his education that year, and he was invited to, and accepted multiple speaking engagements. Rawson nevertheless succumbed to the emotional pressure of reintegrating into a new world while carrying the burden of the realities of war. He died by suicide a few weeks after his twenty-third birthday. His nephew explained that "he knew that they were killing civilians … that was part of what he had difficulty dealing with when he came back, given his strong Christian background." [22] The coroner had reported that Rawson's death was a result of his "failure to completely recover from intensive duties and responsibilities in his war experience." Today we would call this post-traumatic stress disorder (PTSD). Although it took many years, Rawson was finally classified in 2018 as having died from the war and was thus eligible to be recognized with a War Graves Commission gravestone.

I often wonder how Donald was able to negotiate these emotional challenges. On one hand, he was very lonely, writing to many of his friends and family, and never receiving much contact in return. On the other hand, he still managed to pursue his intensive training and bond with his aircrew. And like his grandparents, he persisted in the face of such hardship.

Donald and his fellow crew members had been with the 429 Squadron almost one month; they'd known crews who did not return, and knew that a loss rate of at least five percent could be expected on any single mission. If it wasn't your squadron that lost some crew members on a mission, the word would come from another squadron nearby about their losses. Moreover, many of the men had relatives, like a brother, or friends from home, who lost their lives at the same time, serving somewhere else in the war. It was not unusual to only learn of their loss in a letter from home.

Donald never learned that on a raid to Leverkusen, a Halifax bomber, no. LK950, was seriously damaged by flak, and the aircraft had crashed over the Thames estuary, near Canterbury. The crew bailed out and one member perished. The missing crew member was Alex McEwen, a friend of Donald's from Preston, Ontario, who was stationed at the same Middleton base as Milt Schmidt. Alex and Donald were the two friends pictured together in the newspaper as they arrived at the Bournemouth Depot; Alex was nineteen years old. Sergeant Air Gunner McEwen has no known grave, though his name is inscribed on the Runnymede War Memorial, Englefield Green, Egham, Surrey, England.

Donald was good at math, and like the rest of the airmen, he knew their chances. One day a crew with the experience of twenty or more sorties would be lost, and the next it was a sprog crew. While the loss rates of the rookie crews were always higher, there was no way of knowing whose "turn" it was next. Fear, hope, and anticipation ran through the minds of the aircrew as they waited for their call. Patience was not a notable characteristic in young men, and waiting was their most difficult assignment.

Footnotes Chapter 8

[1] G.H. Adlam, "Source of Strength", in *Rhyme and Reason, A Souvenir Volume of Verse by Canadian Soldier-Poets*, (Canadian Public Relations Services, 1945).

Footnotes cont'd

² Vernon M. White, "Four Years And a Bit, "Y" Depot, Halifax, Nova Scotia": https://www.427squadron.com/book_file/white/four_years_cover.html.

³ White, "Four Years."

⁴ I've always looked for quirky connections between my uncle and myself. On the back of Donald's photo is an article by Scott Young, who was in England reporting for the Canadian Press. Scott is the father of musician Neil Young who lived in Winnipeg and attended a school I visited on many occasions with my own students. I was always a fan of Neil's music and today still play his song "Harvest Moon" on a regular basis.

⁵ Robert Collins, *The Long and The Short and The Tall, An Ordinary Airman's War*, (Western Producer Prairie Books, 1986).

⁶ Spencer Dunmore and William Carter. *Reap the Whirlwind, The Untold Story of 6 Group, Canada's Bomber Force of World War II*, (McClelland & Stewart, 1991): 49.

⁷ Doug Harvey, *Boys, Bombs and Brussel Sprouts*, (McClelland and Stewart Limited, 2013), 33.

⁸ Nick Churchill, "A Minute of Intense Devastation – Bournemouth's Bloodiest Air Raid," *Dorset Life*, April 2013, http://www.dorsetlife.co.uk/2013/04/a-minute-of-intense-devastation-bournemouths-bloodiest-air-raid/

⁹ Doug Harvey, *Boys, Bombs and Brussel Sprouts*, p.13.

¹⁰ This is, again coincidentally, my wife's birthday ten years later.

¹¹ See Dunmore, Reap The Whirlwind, p.50, also see:
https://www.mcmaster.ca/ua/alumni/ww2honourroll/rawson.html.

¹² C.M. Johnston, "Barney Rawson, Discover McMaster's World War II Honour Roll", https://www.mcmaster.ca/ua/alumni/ww2honourroll/rawson.html.

Footnotes cont'd

[13] M. Chapman, "The Wartime Evolution of Flight Training in Canada," *Royal Canadian Air Force Journal*, 5, No. 2, (Spring 2016): 11.

[14] Chapman, "Wartime Evolution," 13.

[15] Dunmore, *Reap The Whirlwind*, 22.

[16] Will Bloch's (J23312) military record.

[17] Tom Hawthorn. "Milt Schmidt: NHL player, coach and GM belonged to fabled Bruins line." *The Globe and Mail*, Toronto, January 30, 2017.

[18] Clarence Simonsen, *RAF & RCAF Aircraft Nose Art In World War II*, (Hikoki Publications Ltd, East Yorkshire, (2001).

[19] From left to right, Tim Wainwright, Don Metz, Vick McGray, Earl Burton, Wil Bloch, Tom McCallum. Photo taken by Don Hogg.

[20] David L Bashow,. *No Prouder Place: Canadians and the Bomber Command Experience 1939-1945*. (Vanwell Publishing Limited, 2005).

[21] See Dr. C.M. Johnston's Project, "Discover McMaster's World War II Honour Roll: Byron N.F. Rawson", https://www.mcmaster.ca/ua/alumni/ww2honourroll/rawson.html.

[22] Mark McNeil, The private war of Wing Commander Barney Rawson, *The Hamilton Spectator*, Sunday, September 23, 2018, https://www.guelphmercury.com/news-story/8917736-the-private-war-of-wing-commander-barney-rawson.

Chapter 9

The Raid on Frankfurt

The evil that men do lives after them;
The good is oft interred with their bones.

– William Shakespeare[1]

Donald had arrived in England on July 17, 1943. Four months later, in November, he was still waiting to be assigned to his first mission. He wrote Mel on the 18th of November, opening with "I received your letter today and was waiting for it." He told Mel that his pilot had completed his second dickey flight that night and he would likely be on the next raid. Donald expected to get a leave on November 29, and he was hoping to come down to visit Mel. It was Donald's last letter, and his words to Mel were prescient: "In fact it is almost sure on the 29th unless something happens." For his leave, Donald was saving money to go to London so that he could go skating. As usual, Donald asked Mel if there were any women down there, and promised to come even if there were none.

Donald and his crew had completed training, and the daily routine was mostly repetition and waiting as they anticipated their first real assignment. Patience is not exactly a resilient quality in young men. It is also harder when you do not know what you are waiting for; anxiety builds and it seems as if time moves more slowly. There are reasons that your doctor has magazines in his reception area. For Donald, in his "waiting room," he tried to keep up regular communication with his friends and family. He continued to write letters and complained about the number he received in return. He told Mel that the mail from home was "piss poor," and that he'd only received one letter in the last three weeks.

Donald's father still worked at Silverwood's Dairy, and a woman from the office would write Donald. She was the wife of a friend of his father, who, like many other women during the war, helped keep the service men overseas informed about the homefront. Donald received letters from the office lady but Mel "certainly had the women writing to him." Given the opportunity, Donald did try to maintain correspondence with some young ladies, like Emela Marczak, who was a member of his church. However, only on occasion did he receive a reply, and he struggled to maintain contact. Even when he did receive a letter, the news from home was never too exciting. Donald learned that his beloved dog, Duke, was hit by a car, and that the local Boy Scout troop granted him a leave of absence. Much to his chagrin, Donald had not been in the Boy Scouts for years.

As they waited, the aircrews had no knowledge of the kind of mission they would be assigned to join. The air squadron's operations and targets were varied. Sometimes they would be given searches to locate and attack sea vessels, other times they could be sent out on "gardening" expeditions. Gardening was the crew's term for the laying of mines at sea, mostly along coastal waters. However, the majority of operations were generally air raids on the German homelands.

At the onset of the war, precision bombing against military

targets such as armaments factories, oil refineries, and air force bases was practiced. The RAF Ruhr offensive was a typical strategy of targeting the military industrial complex. The raids would disrupt the production and movement of materials essential for the operation of the German war efforts. The idea was to destroy the resources necessary to conduct a war, which in turn would force a surrender. However, locating and hitting these targets was much more difficult than expected. The alternative strategy was area bombing which was supported by RCAF commanding officer Arthur Harris, who advocated bombing any structures in the target area to cause as much damage as possible. Area bombing increased casualties among the general population, leaving many wounded and homeless, which was intended to impact the "military, industrial and economic system, and the undermining of the morale of the German people to a point where their capacity for armed resistance is fatally weakened."[2] The value of the area bombing strategy was controversial; war production was only slightly disturbed, while many people died.

Nevertheless, in the face of the bombing raids on Britain and the fight for survival, most felt area bombing was necessary. Harris, for example, was unapologetic:

The aim is the destruction of German cities, the killing of German workers and the disruption of civilized community life throughout Germany. It should be emphasized that the destruction of houses, public utilities, transport and lives; the creation of a refugee problem on an unprecedented scale; and the breakdown of morale both at home and at the battle fronts by fear of extended and intensified bombing are accepted and intended aims of our bombing policy, they are not by-products of attempts to hit factories.[3]

Harris set in motion mass bombing operations, where as many as one thousand bombers flew in air streams over various German cities in night raids, causing tremendous destruction. Harris felt that the strategy of area bombing would bring the Nazis to their knees and prevent a disastrous land invasion. Yet, the Germans held on to defend their land – as the British did – with night fighters, anti-aircraft installations, and a wide range of innovative technological developments. As electronic warfare advanced on both sides of the aerial conflict, many of these developments focused on detecting and scrambling navigational signals.

In the fall of 1943, the bombing of Berlin was part of a primary offensive, and numerous sorties took place. Ten major raids were scheduled for the month of November alone. Four of these raids were planned to attack Berlin with diversionary raids on the cities of Frankfurt and Mannheim. Diversionary raids, held on the same day, were used to misdirect the enemy's defensive systems, drawing fire and resources, such as night fighters, away from the mainstream of bombers. When the flight plans were completed for a specific raid, an operations conference would be held amongst the squadron leaders to review the objectives and tactics. Each squadron would produce a "Mayfly," detailing the resources, planes, and crews that would be available to contribute to the effort. On the day of the raid, the squadrons were abuzz with a nervous aura and urgency. In this environment, the airmen's lives were a mixture of intense risk and endangerment, alongside excruciating boredom and booze. Yesterday, the men might be relaxing in the local pub; today they faced imminent peril and demise.

A major raid on Berlin was planned for November 25, 1943, and was called off at the last minute due to poor weather.

The Raid On Frankfurt

However, the diversionary raid over Frankfurt proceeded as planned. It is not clear why poor weather delayed the raid on Berlin but not Frankfurt. Two hundred and sixty-two planes, mostly Halifaxes, participated in the raid. Donald and his crew were assigned to fly the Halifax Handley bomber serial number JD325. The boys were anxious to begin their first mission, displaying all the usual emotions: anticipation, nervousness, and surely fear.

Initially, the briefings for the Frankfurt raid were set for 1400 hours, but they were delayed until 1800 hours, with takeoff set for the late evening. How would a sprog crew react as they nervously waited to engage in their first mission, only to find it delayed? Waiting was enough of a burden without being told to stand down for another four hours. What do you do? Read a magazine? Play catch or cards? Take-off in the late evening meant you would be up all night, so getting some afternoon rest was probably the best idea. But how do you sleep when you are about to embark on your first mission after over a year of training? Chris Hedges suggests that soldiers in the final moments before the fighting begins "weep, vomit and write last letters home."[4]

By 1800 hours, the men were anxious to receive the details of their assignment. A squadron meeting was held in the "Ops" room, an ordinary hall with large maps hung on a wall board. An officer closed the doors as the tension and curiosity grew, and the roll was called. The names of the crews to be dispatched were recorded on the board, and the pilots answered for their crew. The pilot of Halifax JD 325, Willys Bloch, called out:

"Wainwright!" "McGray!" "McCallum!" "Metz!"

The men, seated together, all answered in turn: "HERE!"

Following roll call, an officer stepped up to the podium and barked, "Gentlemen, your target for tonight's raid is Frankfurt," commanding their attention. On a large map of the UK and Europe, the flight crew could now see lines of red tape illustrating the flight paths from their home base in Leeming to the ultimate objective of Frankfurt. The squadron leader took the floor to outline the main details of the mission. Tonight's path, down the coast to the Thames estuary and crossing the channel towards Schelde in Belgium, was explained to the crews. The altitude was set at 20,000 feet, with an approximate flying time of three hours, ten minutes to the raid objective of Frankfurt. The location of the targets, and how the Pathfinders would mark the targets, was described.

Next, an intelligence officer took the podium and outlined the defense systems that the crew could expect to encounter. Known locations of fighter bases, ground guns, searchlight batteries, and radar were reviewed. Of special note were the instructions for how to spot, identify, and evade the counter attacks of the German night fighters. A briefing in the use of "window"[5] was included, and a weather report – covering temperatures at altitude, cloud cover, wind speed, visibility, and the possibility of icing – was outlined for the anxious crews squirming nervously in their seats.

Finally, the crew was given a briefing in case of being shot down. Being shot down was not a remote possibility; the men all knew crews and friends who did not return from previous missions. Following a crash, three scenarios were possible: you did not survive; you survived and were captured; or you survived and found a way to escape. If you were captured, you became a prisoner of war. Some airmen, after surviving a crash, actually evaded capture, sometimes even making their way back home to England. The assistance you might receive on the ground, from, for example, the French resistance fighters, was explained, and potential escape routes were detailed. The men were given some local currency, small tools, a compass, a map, and some food rations to assist their survival while they evaded internment.

Reality began to set in as the ops meeting concluded. The men gathered their gear and put on their flight suits. The crew members busied themselves with the tasks they repeated a hundred times in training. The gunner checked his guns and cleaned his Perspex window as he prepared his turret. Bombs were retrieved from the ammo dump, and the ground crews assisted in "bombing up" the planes. Rations were stored, and each crew member took care of their own flying kit as they carefully packed a parachute and harness. The aircrew picked up their parachutes, and deadpan humour was often tossed around when someone would yell – "Bring it back if it doesn't open."[6] The absurdity helped calm some nerves among the group, who were mostly in their late teens or early twenties.

As the restless aircrews began to prepare for their mission, memories of training would fill the sprog crews minds. They thought of home, friends, the letters they meant to write, and the ones they were hoping would arrive. The crew kept their eye on the control tower for one of two possible signals: a white flare indicated the operation was cancelled; green meant go. Finally, the men were directed to board their plane, and the aircraft then moved to the end of the runway, lined up in order of takeoff.

As Donald laid in his turret, I wonder what came to his mind, what memories might he recall? One time, while training in Brantford in February, Donald arrived at the streetcar station too late to catch the bus back to the base. A truck stopped and let the men ride in the open back for the five-mile trip back to the base. Donald wrote to his mother to tell her that they froze in the winter weather roaring down the country road. I have also been rumbling down a country road in rural Ontario in the back of an open pickup truck. I am sure it must be a pretty close experience to taxiing towards the runway for takeoff. There is the constant racket of the engine punctuated by the vibration of the bumps and dips in the road. Donald surely thought of that experience and what he was going to write to his mother when he returned from his mission.

Take-offs were often sketchy as an aircraft, burdened with a cargo of bombs and highly flammable fuel, gunned down the runway. The crew, completing their last-minute checks, are given the go ahead signal for takeoff. A final "V" for victory, or a thumbs up for good luck, is saluted by the ground crew as the plane lumbers down the runway for departure.

On this Thursday eve, November 25, 1943, the weather was cloudy and visibility moderate; the time had arrived. The anxious crew, especially the rookies, would have received a word of encouragement from their skipper. "Come on boys, I've been on a couple of these runs, and I came back!" As the plane's speed increased, the crew was likely silent – they had done this part a hundred times in training – but the impending mission loomed large in their deliberations. This was for real. Seventeen crews from the 429 Squadron were assigned to join the mission, and the first plane left the ground at 23:19. Eleven more bombers followed quickly in one or two-minute intervals, then misfortune arrived as three planes in a row failed to take off. One had a taxiing accident in a collision with a aircraft from another squadron, and the other two experienced mechanical failures. Donald's sprog crew was in line behind the three mishaps, which delayed their takeoff until 23:54. Their first mission, initially delayed for four hours, now began with the three aircraft in front of them experiencing complications – a situation that would do nothing to calm rising anxieties as they embarked on their assignment. After what must have felt like an eternity, Donald's crew lifted off, and their mission was underway. The wheels were retracted, one final plane followed them, and the whole group was in the air, flying to join an air stream of 262 bombers.

Donald's crew was a sprog crew; it was their first operation. Chris Hedges describes the psyche of military personnel as they begin to engage in a life-threatening endeavour:

> *All are nearly paralyzed with fright. There is a morbid silence that grips a battlefield in the final moments before the shooting starts, one that sets the back of my own head pounding in pain, wipes away all appetite, and makes my fingers tremble as I ready myself to go forward against logic.*[7]

Alan Soderstrom, an air gunner flying out the Croft base in Yorkshire, reflected on the mixed emotions airmen endured in these circumstances: "No training resembles the situation the crew is in now; they are terrified, near panic, and prepare to bail out."[8] Donald and his fellow crew members were now faced with the reality of war; this was not an exercise.

In an air raid that involved hundreds of aircraft from multiple squadrons, the navigator Hogg would review his metrics carefully as the plane wound its way into the airstream. Three bombers had failed to take off that night, and another two aircraft returned back home early. One because of an equipment failure and another experienced a mid-air collision. The No. 6 429 Squadron started their mission with seventeen planes, but only twelve crews were able to enter the airstream on the pathway to their target. Flying could be physically and mentally arduous, and this demanding scene was repeated on multiple airfields for all squadrons joining the mission.

Following takeoff the crews settled into a routine, as the engines roared continuously, each aviator monitored their own well-being. At high altitudes, crew members could experience a lack of oxygen, and below freezing temperatures brought the danger of frostbite. Flak jackets, and other suitable attire to keep you safe and warm, were cumbersome and often set aside. Donald did not like being uncomfortable, so I am quite sure he slid back into these moments of isolation by recalling freezing in the back of a pickup truck near Brantford. In his own self-deprecating way, he probably thought to write Mel complaining that nothing really changes. He was still cold and alone, and didn't want to dance.

The navigator Hogg was engaged in keeping the plane on the planned route. He gathered data from the electronic system and continuously computed the plane's speed and location to keep it on track to the target. In the case of equipment becoming damaged, the navigator would rely on more traditional methods of navigation, such as dead reckoning and celestial navigation. In dead reckoning, you use an earlier position, plane speed, time, and direction to re-calculate the current position or a future trajectory. Celestial navigation uses the angle to known stars, such as Polaris, to determine longitude and latitude. These ancient methods took navigators time in consulting charts and making mathematical calculations. In other words, if your navigational equipment failed, you were like Christopher Columbus in the sky.

The captain Bloch was flying, assisted by the flight engineer Wainwright, who kept a close watch on fuel, oil, and pressure systems. Any damage or unproductive fuel consumption could impair the return flight home. The wireless operator, Victor McGray, was located just beneath the astrodome. He kept his ears trained on the radio and recorded the messages sent from the home base in Morse code. The mid-upper and rear turret gunners, McCallum and Metz, were isolated from the other crew members in their own turrets for the entire flight. Donald sat alone in his rear turret in freezing temperatures at high altitude. Some gunners removed their Perspex window so they could see more clearly as they scanned the dark skies for enemy planes. They swung their turret and gun from side to side, constantly at the ready in case of attack. As the plane gained altitude, McCallum and Metz peered out their windows in an effort to spot enemy fighters. Initially, they could see other members of the air stream to the side, below, or above them, so they had to be able to identify the planes quickly as friend or foe. If the gunner spotted a night fighter, they warned the pilot to swing or corkscrew to the port or starboard side to avoid fire. In the early morning darkness, the bomber stream pushed on, and the crews took one last look at the vanishing British coastline.

The men may have experienced an odd moment of serenity, in defiance of the engine roar, as the planes began to cross the English Channel. In what seemed to be a peaceful serene evening, the bomber stream, led by the Pathfinders, formed a massive armada as they thundered towards their target. In Donald's Halifax JD325, the navigator Hogg announced the arrival of the European coastline to the crew. German defense forces peppered the coast, and the tranquil crossing dissipated rapidly when searchlights began to cast waves of light across the sky. The Germans manned these defenses rigorously, and the moments of calm and serenity did not last long.

Andrée Peel, a female member of the French Resistance who lived on the coast, recounted that:

"The enemy lost no time in organizing defenses, and the roofs of certain houses near the harbour were manned by soldiers. The violence of the bombing was so great that these soldiers were chained to their guns, so that they could not escape the death-dealing hell which was all around them."[9]

On the night of the Frankfurt mission, diversionary raids were not planned; all of the aircraft were heading straight for their objective. Along this route, the German radar station at Ostend, along the Belgian shoreline, picked up the impending attack at 00:45. The station assessed the force as several hundred airplanes and alerted the Luftwaffe to take to the air.[10] The German controllers, alerted by their radar of an incoming raid, hesitated in choosing whether Mannheim or Frankfurt was the target that evening. They finally guessed correctly that Frankfurt was the target and ordered night fighters from multiple bases, including Florennes and Metz,[11] to the air. In response to the raid, the Nachtjagd, a Luftwaffe air defense division, committed almost three hundred aircraft to engage the bomber stream.

The Allied bomber stream stormed across the European landscape, and the German radar defenses began to see the planes as dots on their monitors. The location of the incoming planes would be determined, and then relayed to the night fighters, who approached the scene from various locations. The smaller swift fighters would attempt to engage an air bomber, attacking it with a steady barrage of flak to damage the plane and bring it down.

Donald kept an eye out for enemy fighters as his pilot Bloch readied the aircraft to perform evasive maneuvers. The nervous tension built, and the air stream advanced into the night on route to their destination. To jam the enemy's radar, the aircrew would scatter aluminum chaff called "window" out of the hatch. The aluminum bits would reflect the radar and confuse the radio operators, who would now be looking at thousands of blips or patches of blurs on their screen.

A companion crew of Donald's, flying in Halifax Handley LK995, was one of the first planes to takeoff for the 429 Squadron. It was also one of the first planes to encounter enemy aircraft on route to the target. The plane was attacked and brought down from an altitude of 4900 meters by the German ace fighter Hans Autenrieth at 2:12 a.m. near the Belgium town of Dinant. Six of the seven crew members survived the crash but were captured, and they spent the rest of the war as prisoners of war (POWs). One of the crew, the rear air gunner, was killed. Pilot David Smith recounted, "the Rear Gunner saw and I believe fired in exchange to two bursts from the fighter which severed all controls."[12] Smith gave the order to abandon, but the intercom had faded out and there was no word from the rear gunner, Robert Davis, who probably never heard the order.

A second German fighter pilot, Hptm Eckhart Wilhelm von Bonin, witnessed Autenrieth's success and entered the bomber stream where he attacked another 429 Squadron Halifax JD411, piloted by V.Y. Haines. Von Bonin recorded the intense encounter in his combat report (*Gefechtsbericht*):

> *"My fire set the enemy's aircraft and starboard engines ablaze. The aircraft fell away in flames."* The plane crashed near Olzheim near the German Belgium border. All seven airmen perished.[13]

In the next twenty minutes, von Bonin brought down another two aircraft in the Frankfurt air raid bomber stream from the 78 and 97 Squadrons. As the planes approached their target, over ninety night fighters arrived in defense of the German territory. They faced strong head winds, and with the jamming of their radar, many arrived late.

In an air encounter, there would be evasive actions and counter actions, taken by both sides. As technology advanced the conflict grew more complicated. However, in some cases gaining an advantage over the enemy was more a matter of implementing a more clever scheme. Operation Corona, a program used to confuse German defenses, was introduced just as Donald arrived at Leeming in October 1943. In Operation Corona, German radio communications were intercepted by the Allied Forces, which permitted intelligence to determine how the German night fighters were responding to the raid. Wireless operators, mostly male German Jews who had fled Nazi Germany, and who spoke the language fluently, impersonated the enemy Luftwaffe operators and communicated incorrect information to the night fighter pilots to direct them away from the bomber stream.

In response, the Germans employed female operators to communicate directions to the night fighters. In turn, the Allied Forces engaged some female operators as well. Women like Claire Dyment,[14] a Jewish immigrant from Poland, stepped into service to relay confusing messages to the night fighter pilots. In the German analysis of the November 26 raid on Frankfurt, it was reported that "it is impossible to distinguish between the commentaries given by friend and foe."[15] Instructions would be received by some of the night fighter pilots to land their plane; instructions given by female voices "completely free of any accent."[16] The German response in future raids was to play

Carnival music in the background when planes were over the Rheinland. Over Berlin they played the Prussian marches, and over Vienna it was Mozart.

The tension in the sky, and in the crew, increased as the target drew near. The navigational experts, known as the Pathfinders, were the first to arrive at the objectives. They would mark the locations for bombing with coloured indicators, so the bomb aimers could easily locate their targets and release the bombs. At three a.m. on November 26, 1943, Donald's bomber stream approached the target area at approximately 20,000 feet altitude. Visibility was poor, with clouds up to 15,000 feet. As the crew arrived, they encountered the German defenses in the target area of Frankfurt. Captain Arbuckle, flying the Halifax Handley bomber JD274, reported "Fairly heavy searchlights from Mannheim to the target were supported by medium to heavy flak."[17] The powerful beams flashed by the bombers, attempting to blind them as the anti-aircraft batteries targeted them for destruction. The bombers tried to elude the endless flak barrage with various maneuvers to avoid the intense onslaught.

Donald's crew were experiencing their first mission. The pilot, Bloch, had been a crew member on two "dickey flights," and now captained a nervous crew in a theatre filled with chaotic flying through torrid skies of searchlights, flak, and arresting mayhem. He would shout out commands and maintain direct communication with the bomb aimer, who was busy trying to locate his targets. A sprog crew flying in such mayhem would prove to be a frightening challenge. Flight Lieutenant J.D. Pattison, a former fighter pilot and Battle of Britain veteran, described his first raid as a "strange sight to the novice."

> *The target area was brilliantly lit up by flares which were being shot up from the ground to aid the night fighters by silhouetting the bombers against the low cloud and haze. Off our starboard bow, as we ran in to bomb, there was a huge cone made up of about seventy-five searchlights and reaching up to over 15,000 feet. Into this cone, Flak was being pumped by many guns in the area ... The flares, fires, and searchlights made it very uncomfortable around the target as it was lit up like day. One feels so conspicuous in a bomber which has neither darkness nor cloud to hide in.*[18]

Imagine being out in the darkness of night in a remote location. Someone pulls out their flashlight and points it upward at their chin as they begin to tell a scary story. At the climax of the story, they wave their hand violently, screaming "the call is coming from inside the house!" The onlookers jump in horror, then all collapse in laughter. For Donald and crew, the story being played out brought the sudden horror and chill, but no laughter. There was only constant terror as flak batteries blasted anti-aircraft fire from all directions while light pierced the murky skies. In the operational activities of the Royal Canadian Air Force, the flight over the target area is described as:

> *The searchlights surrounding the objective are filling the sky with their long white fingers trying to pick out the bombers. The clear blue master searchlight points, the others follow; again the kite is coned just as it is ready to begin the straight and level bombing run. The pilot jinks and finally escapes the lights and the tons of flak thrown up. Heavy flak, this time, with its awful c-l-u-m-p and death-dealing power.*[19]

The wave of incoming bombers would be illuminated by the searchlights as targets for a barrage of ground fire. In his very first mission, the young Donald's job would be to manage his gun turret while tracking enemy attacks and calling out evasive maneuvers to his pilot as the planes stormed nearby. Pilots would immediately go into a deep dive to avoid being hit. If the dive was too steep and they couldn't pull out, they could crash, or at times collide with another plane. The searing sounds of the frenzied night were punctuated by rapid ground fire, sirens blaring as engines droned. The reverberation of nearby bombers and night fighters ruled the early morning darkness.

The searchlights that had coned the planes were often operated by young teens commonly called the *Flakhelfers* (literally anti-aircraft helpers). The Flakhelfers were young male students, fourteen or fifteen years of age, who were drafted into service and supervised by the Hitler Youth program. As a fourteen-year-old in Canada, Donald had entered the world of work while pursuing his passions of playing hockey, partying with friends, and chasing young ladies in the emerging teenage culture in North America. In contrast, the Flakhelfers were fourteen-year-olds who were removed from their adolescence and forced into a perilous service where they found themselves targets of an enemy attack.

One of the most astonishing young men drafted into this service was Joseph Alois Ratzinger. Ratzinger, whose family despised the Nazis, was "an unenthusiastic member who refused to attend meetings"[20] and who later deserted back to his family's home as the war came to an end. In the years to come, Ratzinger became better known by his service in the Catholic faith as Pope Benedict XVI.

As the Flakhelfers lit up the skies, several night fighters shot down three Halifaxes and severely damaged another plane from the 419 Squadron. Despite this, it was reported to be a disappointing night for the Nachtjagd, as a number of German night fighters had been fooled by the Operation Corona ladies. This was one more silent – or perhaps not so silent – role that women played in the war. Nine German pilots were lost in the combat, and several more planes experienced engine failure and icing damage. It seemed that neither side was very satisfied with the raid. In the RCAF squadron reports, most pilots claimed the raid was very difficult to assess, and few bombs landed on their targets.

Following the chaos over Frankfurt, most of the planes and their aircrews survived. Yet the mission was only half over: the boys now had to find their way home.

Footnotes Chapter 9

[1] From Shakespeare's Julius Caesar.

[2] Brereton Greenhous, *The Official History of the Royal Canadian Air Force, volume III, The Crucible of War 1939-1945*, (University of Toronto Press, 1994): 657.

[3] Sir Arthur Harris, 25 October 1943, quoted in Greenhous, *The Crucible of War*, p. 725.

[4] Chris Hedges, *War is a Force That Gives Us Meaning* (Anchor Books, 2003): 38.

[5] "Window" was a radar deflection strategy.

[6] Lisa Jean Russ, *Last Flight to Stuttgart: Searching for the Bomber Boys of Lancaster EQ-P* (Heritage House, 2018): 9.

[7] Chris Hedges, *War is a Force*, 38.

[8] Alan Soderstrom, "Night Raid on Happy Valley", http://www.rcaf434squadron.com/happy-valley/

[9] Peel, Andrée. *Miracles Do Happen.*(Loebertas, 2011): 321.

The Raid On Frankfurt

Footnotes cont'd

[10] Theo Boiten, *Nachtjagd Combat Archive, 1943 Part 3*, (Red Kite, 2018): 80.

[11] Metz is a city in France, the irony is not lost to me.

[12] Archive Report: Allied Forces, 25/26.11.1943 No 429 Squadron Halifax V LK995, https://aircrewremembered.com/smith-david.html.

[13] Recorded in von Bonin's Gefechtsbericht (combat report) as reported in Boiten, `*Nachtjagd Combat Archive*..80-81, The seven are V.Y. Haines, S. Monorieff, H. Copping, A.W. Roberts, W.H. Lowe, D. Scott, and A.T, Gardiner.

[14] T.B. Austin, "CLAIRE'S STORY," https://www.secret-ww2.net/operation-corona-claires-story.

[15] Boiten, *Nachtjagd Combat Archive, 1943 Part 3*, 80–81.

[16] Boiten, *Nachtjagd Combat Archive, 1943 Part 3*, 80–81.

[17] Operational Record Book, 429 Squadron, November 1943, *The National Archives*, reference AIR 27/1852/2.

[18] Brereton Greenhous, *The Official History of the Royal Canadian Air Force, volume III, The Crucible of War 1939-1945*, (University of Toronto Press, 1994): 583.

[19] *The R.C.A.F. Overseas: The Fifth Year*, (Toronto Oxford University Press, 1945): 18.

[20] John Thornton, and Susan Varenne, *The Essential Pope Benedict XVI: His Central Writings and Speeches*, (Harper One, 2009).

Chapter 10

La Terre Rouge

Upon a distant hillside, there stands a linden tree.

– Franz Schubert

The Allied bombing raid on Frankfurt took place in the early morning hours of November 26, 1943. As the planes entered the bomber stream and crossed the English Channel, they were picked up by the coastal radar, and the German defense systems were kicked into action. Aircraft interceptors managed to take down a few planes, but the vast majority headed on to their target. Following the raid, the final challenge was the flight home. After the bombing run concluded, Luftwaffe night fighters (the Nachtjagd) would follow the invaders, frantically chasing them on their way back home, sometimes right up to British territory. Apart from the impending threat of the Nachtjagd night fighters chasing aircrews on a cross country pursuit home, planes could also experience mechanical failure due to flak or serious collision damage. Even after the aircraft had crossed the English Channel, the landing had to be made in sometimes perilous weather conditions. Vernon White was a bomb aimer who followed a similar training path as Donald, and who was also posted at Leeming in 1943. He described one of his flights home from a bombing run being chased by a night fighter. "The Halifax was holed twenty times, both inboard engines were hit but luckily didn't conk, while the starboard rudder, fuselage, and main plane also took a severe beating."[1] They were constantly bombarded with flak that was "like hail," and at one time the pilot pitched the plane and dropped from 19,000 ft to 13,000 ft in an evasive maneuver. The Halifax plane's rear rudder controls were severely damaged, but the pilot managed to bring the crew in for a "good landing." Damage to a plane could cause crash landings, and in some cases, pilots had to abort the landing completely to bail in the open seas, hoping to be rescued.

White described a good landing as "one that you can walk away from." Once landed, the exhausted aircrew were picked up and escorted to the debriefing room to meet with RCAF intelligence officers. Following his bombing operation, White re-counted:

"The boys who took to the air six hours earlier are nowhere to be seen, their place has been taken by old, disillusioned, dirty men with lack-lustre eyes and heavy hands. One or two drowse, even fall asleep; the rest talk quietly or just sit."[2]

The crews would file a combat report on the weather, along with details of their mission such as air defenses, night fighter engagements, and their records of the bombing locations. As they completed their report and headed to breakfast, the men became aware of the day's losses. The entire raid consisted of 262 bombers and twelve crews were lost that evening. The rate of loss (4.6 per cent) was considered a respectable liability in the eyes of the Bomber Command. The No. 6 Group assigned eighty-eight aircraft to the mission and eighty-two returned safely. The different squadrons of the No. 6 Group all had their up and down days as the bombing missions became a regular undertaking. The losses, while spread across the No. 6 Group, could be sporadic within each squadron. Commanding Officer C.E. Harris[3] of the 434 Squadron wrote in his Operational Report that, "It was really something to have all our A/C and crews return safely from an ops trip after the bad luck of the last few weeks, so everyone was very elated." The 434 Squadron had lost several crews leading up to the Frankfurt raid, but on that evening, and on the next evening's raid on Stuttgart, the 434 squadron again had no losses. The men were ecstatic, and Harris reported "great rejoicing" for having no losses on two consecutive missions as "almost a record on this squadron." The men of the 434 celebrated with a squadron trip by bus and train to Harrogate for an evening of enjoyment, not returning to camp until past midnight. For the young men it was truly a life of bombing, heartbreak, boredom, or booze.

While the men of the 434 had reason to celebrate, the other RCAF squadrons all experienced damages. The 434 had been given a reprieve, but it was the turn of Squadrons 429 and 431 to endure their fatalities. Both squadrons had experienced just a few casualties over the previous three months. However, on this night, Donald's 429 Squadron lost three planes, and the 431 Squadron suffered two more. In total, these two squadrons lost five of the six crews missing from the eighty-eight aircrews sent on the assignment from the No. 6 Group. As depressing as it could be losing your comrades, and even a close friend, the men learned to deal with their grief. John Martin was a twenty-one-year-old wireless operator whose plane was taken down over Germany during a bombing run to Berlin. Surviving the crash and writing of his experiences, he reflected on the pain and sorrow of dealing with the loss of members of your squadron:

> *When you heard that someone you knew hadn't come back you just had to bury your thoughts. There was no use asking what had happened because you knew you wouldn't get an answer. That's it; you just had to take it. The only good thing was, you didn't have long to think about it because the next mission always came – if you were lucky, that is.*[4]

"Just having to take it" was a pain that many men carried for the rest of their lives. For most, the sadness and sorrow were buried within. Others, like Barney Rawson, held on to their suffering through post-traumatic stress disorder (PTSD), unrecognized and alone.

In the 429 Squadron's combat report for the night raid of November 25/26, the bomber crews who were not accounted for were listed as "Aircraft failed to return from this mission." The overall achievements of the Bomber Command during the war came at a high price. Forty-five percent of the airmen who joined the Command lost their lives, six percent were seriously injured, and another eight percent became prisoners of war.[5] No doubt, with the addition of those who suffered mentally, the loss was devastating. Still, the youthful airmen served and stood in line to take their turn at bringing peace back to the world.

In the early morning hours of November 26, 1943, twelve aircraft never made it back home. While some were intercepted in the air stream, the real conflict escalated as the bombers entered and then tried to escape the target area. As the planes were "coned" by powerful searchlights, they would become targets for flak batteries guarding the city. Additionally, scores of Luftwaffe night fighters took to the skies to engage the bombers in a cat-and-mouse struggle as the aircraft dodged shrapnel with evasive maneuvers such as a corkscrew or spin-dive. The bombing run only lasted about twenty minutes, and the planes were quick to clear the area. However, many were chased by a night fighter as they fled, sometimes for several hours. The RCAF Overseas described the encounters between the Allied bombers and the swift Luftwaffe planes:

> *Suddenly a shrill "Fighter!" breaks the silence and the excitement really starts. Evasive action begins and all guns start chattering as the swiftly moving battle is waged. Ping, ping, as machine-gun bursts pierce the fuselage or the wings. If the crew are unlucky they cop a cannon shell and fire breaks out. As the pilot throws the four-engined monster around, crew members work madly to put out the fire while the gunners still engage the night fighter.*[6]

In the combat report for the mission filed by Pilot H.R. Dow of the 434 Squadron, he reported that his rear gunner sighted an enemy aircraft dead astern. Pilot Dow countered by performing combat maneuvers, corkscrewing and driving turns, as the Rear Gunner fired rapidly at the approaching fighter. The enemy followed, shadowing Dow and his crew as they fled the airspace over Frankfurt.

Night fighters would often try to fly below the bombers, where they could not be seen, with a goal of firing into the belly of the plane. Any harm to the aircraft would make the journey home more difficult and landing treacherous. Engine failure, wing damage, or interference with the plane's mechanisms, such as the heating circuit, would put the crew in jeopardy. The icy temperatures at 20,000 feet could freeze their limbs and disable their communication systems. If the plane still had bombs, they could ignite, and everyone would be lost. Even after releasing their bombs, the aircraft, still carrying a load of fuel, was subject to a fierce explosion and fire.

The aircraft were often chased off course by these night fighters, and could experience difficulty flying a direct route home in poor weather conditions. Donald was flying in the Handley Halifax JD325 piloted by Willys Bloch. The plane, chased by German night fighters, was spotted by eyewitnesses near the town of Carignan at the French-Belgian border; it was on fire as it circled around and tried to land, or so it seemed. Vernon White, who was taken POW in a previous raid, described the chaos in his Halifax after being struck by flak:

There was a tremendous jolt and a series of dull sounding explosions felt throughout the aircraft. The port engines were immediately put out of action and the pilot's instruments begin to spin madly ... the crew did not know whether they had been hit by flak or cannon from a night fighter ... the pilot activated the fire extinguishers, feathered the propellers in the two port engines, and tried to bring the aircraft under control with the two starboard engines.[7]

White could see that his plane was losing altitude as the pilot cried "Bail out, Bail out!" over the intercom. Some of the aircrew were having problems opening the escape hatch, and the navigator was such a big guy that he was barely able to squeeze through the opening. White bailed and was able to open his parachute. He recounted as he descended to the ground that he thought of his family and "perhaps incongruously, that he had a date with a Land Army girl the following Saturday." Donald, and the rest of the aircrew of Halifax JD325, had no such luck bailing from their plane. Bloch may have tried some evasive actions, but their demise was rapid as no one had prepared for evacuating the plane by parachute. I have no doubt that Donald, in his last few moments, thought of his mother, and perhaps a dance he might have tried. Finally, the plane crashed on the hillside called Mount Tilleul near the Linden tree, a local landmark. Stanislas, in nearby Sedan, and the people of Carignan jumped from their beds. They checked on their children, but kept the lights off and curtains closed. They could hear the Gestapo roar in on their motorcycles. The flames grew.

A local woman, Mme Berriot,[8] heard the impending crash and immediately went outside to find the location of the plane. Seeing the flames on the hill she advanced quickly to the scene. Berriot was the first person in the vicinity of the crash and about a half kilometer from the burning aircraft she ran into a young man, slightly more than six feet tall she thought, with light brown hair, hastily walking away from the wreckage. His hair was burned, and his face blackened with oil and soot. The airman was disoriented, and he wore a long trench coat and a pair of Irving trousers. Mme Berriot then quickly cleaned his face with a handkerchief and removed the Irving trousers, which she later hid in the nearby cemetery. The crash survivor wore blue-grey battledress trousers under his Irvings. He spoke some French, but very poorly, and asked which direction was Belgium. He refused further help as the Gestapo was just arriving on the scene, and hurriedly made off in the direction of the Belgian border. Mme Berriot quickly fled the crash area as the Gestapo approached; the next day she burned the survivor's Irving trousers that she had hid in the cemetery.

Leaving the crash scene, Mme Berriot conveyed the incident to Henry Vin, chief of the regional Maquis. The Maquis were French resistance fighters during the Nazi occupation.

They often could be found hiding out in rural areas to avoid capture and expulsion to Germany, and into forced labour. The Maquis were active allies in providing emergency assistance to downed airmen. It is thought that about fifteen percent of the Maquis were young women like Mme Berriot. Although I do not know the occupation of Mme Berriot, many of the young female Maquis were schoolteachers. As she was an assistant to

Henri Vin[9] was born in Carignan in 1922; he was the same age as Donald. Like Donald, Henri was seventeen when the war began. As the war progressed, he was driven underground, and his heroism saw him rise to a commander of the Maquis. Vin had become a teacher trainee in nearby Sedan, and later started to work for the SNCF, the French railway company. Vin was recruited into the Maquis by Robert Briffaut,[10] also born in 1922, a college student in Sedan who went underground to avoid the *Service du Travail Obligatoire* (STO). Briffaut knew Vin's sister Jeanne, and he had initially recruited Vin to provide information about the routing and supply movement of the Germans by rail. In 1942, Vin was called to the STO. Instead of serving in the STO, he joined the underground group led by Briffaut. The group found refuge in the forest region nearby the Belgian border between Carignan and Florenville (the Bois du Banel).

Henri was given the pseudonym, "Petitjean," and he became the head of the intelligence service of the Maquis du Banel. This branch of the Maquis assisted Allied Forces, downed in France, who were trying to evade capture. After the war, Vin returned to teaching, became a college professor, and was elected mayor in the town of Margut, near Carignan. He was a popular politician, re-elected four times and widely recognized for his heroic endeavours during the war.

Mme Berriot was Henry Vin's assistant. Although women made up only fifteen percent of the Maquis, they played a critical role and were widely unrecognized for their bravery. As the Germans made great efforts to forcibly draft young Frenchmen into the STO, the young men sought shelter underground and turned their resistance into clandestine operations, most often carried out in the dead of night. Women, however, could usually move about more freely, passing information gathered from the German movements to the Maquis, and often on to Britain. They even helped British spies who parachuted into France to perform secretive operations. The women, many very young, also helped Allied soldiers escape prisoner of war camps by coordinating access to boats on the western shore to transport them home.

A big part of the young women's efforts included aiding airmen who were shot down. They were well trained; Andrée Peel,[11] who took the code name "Rose", often helped downed airmen near her home on the west coast of France. She described that her "first job was to fold up the parachute and bury or burn it, and then to find jackets and trousers for the men to wear instead of their uniforms."[12] This was exactly the procedure that Mme Berriot took on as she arrived at the scene of Donald's crash. Andrée would also deliver secret messages, such as the location of German troops; she guided aircraft landings of secret agents from United Kingdom and escorted escapees to boats for return to the UK. If they could, these young women hid the downed airmen in friendly homes and provided clothing, food, shelter, and medical assistance. Mme Berriot was ready to perform these duties for Donald and his fellow crew as they crashed near her home in Carignan. Endangering her own life as the Gestapo rapidly approached, she still assisted the lone survivor in his escape.

Women like Mme Berriot performed their duties with full knowledge of the consequences if they were caught – and many were tragically caught. The ladies who were captured were not spared by their Nazi interrogators. After being betrayed by a colleague, who was forced to watch his family being tortured, Andrée Peel was arrested and stripped naked. She described her ordeal:

They threw me into a huge metal bathtub, then used their boots to weigh down my body and keep me under the water. When I was about to expire, they seized me by my hair and dragged me out of the water so that I could breathe. As soon as they thought that my life was no longer in danger, they plunged me in again. I don't know how many times they repeated the performance before the officer said: "Will you speak or not?" "But I've nothing to say." His irritation reached a crisis point. He gave another signal and one of the SS soldiers took me by my hair and forced me to kneel while he struck my throat over and over again, knocking me most brutally against the iron rim of the bathtub. My gullet was displaced to the right and my tonsils were crushed and severed. The pain was atrocious. I was unable to swallow my saliva and I found I was swallowing my crushed tonsils. I don't know how my vocal cords were not destroyed.[13]

Andrée, blackened and severely bruised, exemplifying the heroic courage of the women of the Maquis, still refused to speak, and was sent to prison in Germany. Mme Berriot in Carignan did not accidentally stumble into Donald's crash site. She was prepared for her service, and while she was not able to save Donald and the other members of the aircrew who did not survive the crash, she arrived on the scene in a moment trying to assist the lone survivor. The identity of the lone survivor is still unknown. As he was never found, it was surmised that he was later killed by the enemy and buried in an isolated grave some distance from the scene of the crash. I did find some evidence, never officially acknowledged, that the surviving member was Victor McGray. In the National Archives of Great Britain, there are record cards of British and Commonwealth prisoners of war from the Second World War. These cards, written in German, contain the details of Allied airmen whose bodies were found in German occupied territory. The cards, originally German records, include varying amounts of POW information including date and place of capture, internment camp, and sometimes even fingerprints and photographs. In this archive I found a card for Victor McGray that contains his rank, regiment (429 Squadron), his serial number, and date of death (26/11/1943). No further information is listed. Since a German-recorded card exists, it is quite likely that McGray was the survivor of the crash, and that he was captured shortly after and killed, but not buried in Carignan.

In the early dawn, many people from the local community, including young Stanislas Greb from Sedan, began to gather near the crash site. The Gestapo was also beginning to assemble to search the plane, and they warned the people, who were bringing flowers, to leave the area immediately. The Mayor of Carignan, Monsieur Colle, arrived and yelled for the bystanders to disperse or they may be shot. The mayor collected the mutilated bodies of the airmen, and in a cart pulled by two oxen, they descended the hill to the nearby cemetery. The Germans swiftly dug four graves and placed the remains of the aviators in the graves. The coffins were covered with earth, the men were now buried. The communal graves were exhumed following the war, and it was reported that "the jumbled remains of a crew have been haphazardly shovelled into the coffins by the

Germans without any attempt at separation into individual crew members ... three in one, two in another, and one in each of the remaining two graves."[14] One box contained a severed arm, which wore an identity bracelet labelled Burton. Shortly after the war was over an investigation was conducted to try to determine the identity of the other airmen and to label their graves appropriately. The body of McCallum was positively identified, and he was re-buried in his own grave. But the small box said to contain a hand with Burton's identity bracelet was never located. The cemetery guardian reported to the investigators that he discredits this story, and that it was a well-known fact that the mayor had possession of this bracelet. It was said that Mayor Colle was later assassinated for collaborating with the Germans.

Over the years, the plane remained on the hill, now known as La Terre Rouge. The plane, and the crash site, became a relic that children would explore right up into the 1950s. A local gentleman, born in 1942, reported to me that he lived in the village of Blagny, near Carignan. When he was eight or nine years old, he would go to the crash site with some friends and pick up small pieces of debris such as Plexiglas, which they would burn. He described some of his adventures to me:

> *The combustion gave off a black smoke and had a characteristic smell that I have not forgotten. Subsequently, we dug around the impact and we unearthed a lot of debris of mechanical parts. I even remember finding a radio headset with its earphones, but what we mostly found were machine gun cartridges similar to those of the English Lee-Enfield rifle. We had fun burning the powder which was in the form of fine sticks of nitro-cellulose.*[15]

Another young eyewitness, who was seven years old at the time, remembered that the German soldiers with their dogs guarded the wreck the day after the crash. Later, he saw some Plexiglas, a bullet, and a piece of metal, painted black on one side and covered in blood, in the possession of a neighbour.[16] While the crash was a center of curiosity to the children of the 1950s, who knew little of war, the people of Carignan cared deeply for the lost airmen who had been buried in their small cemetery. The graves are now marked by the Commonwealth War Graves Commission with appropriate headstones. The site has been maintained and graced with flowers for over seventy years.

The war was now at an end for Donald and his crew. On his grave it is marked that he was nineteen years old. A young man, searching for his place in the world, found his permanent resting place on a serene hillside in rural France.

As I reflect on my identity, my name, and namesake, the generational disparity is not lost on me. How different were we? At nineteen years of age, I was living freely, working as a lifeguard at the YMCA, even enjoying the occasional dance. I had my own travels and adventures. I hitchhiked across Canada, the United States, and Mexico. For a while, I wandered through the poor rural areas of Guatemala hanging out with young men from the United States who were dodging the draft during the Vietnam era. We sang anti-war anthems together.

What's in a name? I still needed to answer the question. As I discovered where my uncle was laid to rest, there was still one more thing for me to do. Visit him.

Footnotes Chapter 10

[1] Bert Wemp, "Toronto Flyer Takes Plane alone through Essen Barrage," *The Toronto Telegram*, June 18, 1943, as quoted in Vernon M. White, "Four Years And a Bit, "Y" Depot, Halifax, Nova Scotia", https://www.427squadron.com/book_file/white/four_years_cover.html.

[2] The R.C.A.F. Overseas, The Fifth Year, (Toronto Oxford University Press, 1945): 20.

[3] Operations Record Book, AIR 27/1865/7, *National Archives*.

[4] John Martin, *A Raid over Berlin*, (Parthian Books, June 2019): 15.

[5] For details see the Bomber Command Museum:
https://www.bombercommandmuseum.ca/bomber-command/bomber-commands-losses/

[6] *The R.C.A.F. Overseas, The Fifth Year*, (Toronto Oxford University Press, 1945): 19.

[7] White, Vernon, "Four Years and a Bit, 427 Squadron, Leeming Yorkshire,"
https://www.427squadron.com/book_file/white/four_years_intro.html.

[8] Mme Berriot was interviewed on November 20th, 1946, by F/Lt. Aptroot of the No. 1 Missing Research and Enquiry Unit.

[9] Henri Vin, "Biography of the Fifth Republic," http://www2.assemblee-nationale.fr/sycomore/fiche/%28num_dept%29/11058.

[10] Roger Orianne, "Sedan: memories of resistance fighters", *Ardennes Week*," Sept 2012,
https://www.lasemainedesardennes.fr/sedan/2012/09/08/sedan-souvenirs-de-resistants/.

[11] Peel, Andrée. *Miracles Do Happen,* (Loebertas, 2011).

[12] Peel, Andrée. *Miracles Do Happen,* (Loebertas, 2011): 351.

[13] Peel, Andrée. *Miracles Do Happen,* (Loebertas, 2011): 514.

Footnotes cont'd

[14] E.J. Dawes, Exhumation report. Members of the 429 Squadron who perished on November 26, 1943, near Carignan, France are Willys Roland Bloch, Earl Allen Burton, Donald Allan Hogg, Peter Thompson McCallum, Victor Wallace McGray, Donald James Metz, and Timothy Wainwright.

[15] Personal letter to me via Francis Raymond, secretary of the neighbouring historical and artistic circle.

[16] Anonymous:https://www.britmodeller.com/forums/index.php?/topic/234909641-finding-a-halifax/&tab=comments#comment-930744

Chapter 11

My Journey

Remember that you and I made this journey together to a place where there was nowhere left to go.

— Jhumpa Lahiri, The Namesake

I was standing in the cold November wind with my family at a solemn Remembrance Day service when I heard a resonant voice announce my name on the loudspeaker. I think I was four, maybe five years old, and as a precocious, earnest young child, I immediately questioned my mother:

"Who called me?"

"Shhhh …" I was told.

I repeated, "Why did they call my name?"

"SHHH! …" I was told, more adamantly this time.

"Look … Watch!" my mother insisted.

I saw my grandmother, escorted by my father and my two uncles, Ivan and Floyd. She shuffled slowly, carrying a wreath, and placed it, with tears in her eyes, on the Cenotaph stairs, alongside numerous other wreaths. Later that day, as the family gathered at Grandma's, I learned for the first time that I had another uncle, and I had been given his name. I was told that he died in a war and is no longer with us. Nothing more.

I often wondered about the uncle who I never met or knew, yet whose name I carried. Years went by, his memory waned and I would periodically ask my parents about him. No pictures were hung on the wall; no acknowledgements were ever made of his birthday, the anniversary of his demise, or where he was laid to rest. My father did not want to talk about his brother and would change the subject if I brought it up throughout the years. Finally, on my fourteenth birthday, my father gave me my uncle's picture and medals: the War Medal 1939–1945, which was awarded to all full-time service members, the Canadian voluntary service medal, the 1939–1945 Star awarded for service in the RCAF Bomber Command, and the Air Crew Europe Star, awarded for operational flying from the UK over Europe. Yet, I still did not have any answers to my curiosity about who this person was, what he liked to do, and how he died.

As the time went by, my curiosity would ebb and flow unevenly. I thought about my uncle occasionally when I heard my name announced formally at school, like the Remembrance Day service. Over the years, I was asked on multiple occasions if I was related to Don Metz. My interest would suddenly intensify – someone knew my uncle! – then quickly fade when I realized I was being asked if I was related to Don Metz, a professional hockey player for the Toronto Maple Leafs in the late 1940s and early 1950s. The pro hockey player named Don

Metz was no relation of mine, but I was often asked about him many times. Even though my uncle loved hockey and carried his skates with him everywhere, his role in the game was only to clean the ice.

There was one exception. When I was nineteen, I worked at a residential boys' camp for the YMCA. The age of the campers was seven to twelve years old. The thirteen to fourteen-year-olds who wished to attend the camp were assigned to be Junior Leaders who helped supervise the younger campers. However, there was a group of thirteen to fifteen-year-old boys, mostly from the inner city, who were not capable of handling those duties and who were assigned to their own cabin. I was appointed to mentor this challenging group of youths as their camp counsellor. They could be a motley crew, usually difficult to control, and they became known at camp as Metz's Monsters. I tried many strategies to make them feel and act responsibly – not always successfully. I would take them hiking around the lake and swimming in a location outside of the camp's boundary as a stealth adventure, just to get them away from the younger ones. I would find fun, practical games they could play – hide and seek with the younger campers, and the occasional water balloon fight with some friendly senior counsellors – so they could learn how to have a good time without the activity degenerating into fist fighting.

At suppertime we ate together at a table in the mess hall, and every day we were given a jug of fruit juice to share as a group. Because the boys were older than the other kids, there was never enough juice to go around, and disputes would always emerge. I would request an extra jug, but the three teenage girls who worked in the kitchen informed me that they were only allowed to set one jug per table. I was friendly with one of the girls, Lynn, and wanted to make the point that we really needed more to drink. So, one day I decided to play a prank to make my case, tease Lynn a bit, and get an extra jug of juice. I poured a glass of juice, laced it with vinegar, and called Lynn to check out the problem with it. She came to the table, tried the juice, and choked as she took a drink. Lynn apologized profusely for such a poor tasting beverage and went to retrieve us a new jug of juice. The Monsters were laughing hilariously as one of the boys carried the spiked glass of juice back to the kitchen with Lynn. He chatted with her briefly, then Lynn asked me to come to the kitchen so she could get me another jug of juice. I gave a thumbs up to the Monsters as they cheered for more drinks, not yet knowing that they had turned me in.

Dinner that night was spaghetti, and it was laid out in the kitchen in large bowls with meatballs and sauce. As I entered the kitchen, Lynn shouted at me, "How dare you, Don Metz!" and dumped a bowl of spaghetti over my head. I know karma is a b**tch and I deserved every last noodle I was wearing. The Monsters loved it, especially since from then on we got an extra jug of juice.

Another person, the head cook Bob, an older chap, watched the whole scene unfold in the kitchen. He joined in the laughter and afterwards approached me, asking, "Are you related to the Don Metz who lived down on Benton Street?" My demeanour transformed instantly; no one had ever asked me this before, and I had been waiting to say my entire life, "Yes, Yes, I am! Did you know him? Were you a friend?" Bob said that he knew him when they were teenagers. I pleaded, "Can you tell me about him, please, anything." Bob replied, "We have supper to finish first, so why don't you come to my cabin later this evening and we'll chat?"

Later that evening I dropped by Bob's cabin, and he invited me to join him for a drink. He pulled out a twelve pack of beer and opened one for me and one for himself. I immediately felt that he certainly knew my uncle's habits. I asked him, "What did you know about my Uncle Donald?" He told me that "Donnie" was a real character. They would play hockey outdoors in the winter at the park, and he saw him at dances in the Granite Club. Bob said my uncle always had a wicked, and sometimes "wicked", sense of humour. I asked about the dances, since I was interested in music, and he said Don didn't do much there but hang around with the boys in the corner, ogling the girls. His best friend was Mel, who was usually with him, and they were constantly gabbing about this or that, and usually which girls they'd like to check out.

I asked Bob some more specific questions about my uncle, such as what was his favourite movie, did they go to school together, did he visit my uncle at home, did he know my dad, and many more queries. However, Bob didn't know much more, and it turned out that he was mostly a lonely old man interested in having someone to drink with and talk to for a while. After a couple more beers and an array of tangential information, I thanked him for the information and went on my way. I now had some things about my uncle to think about: we both liked beer, played hockey, and hung out in the corner at the dance hall.

Later, I moved west to Winnipeg, Manitoba and it was not unusual to be asked again if I was related to Don Metz. But it always turned out to be the NHL hockey player for Toronto, Don Metz, who along with his older brother Nick, was born in Saskatchewan. Each time, I had wished it had brought back recollections of my own hockey-loving uncle, but the only memories I carried was of my grandmother laying the wreath on Remembrance Day, my name being called, and my brief conversation with Bob. Nothing much changed over the next forty years.

In 2006, my mother passed away, and I came home for her funeral. Following the church service, a woman approached me and asked if I was Don Metz. I said yes, fully expecting the next query to be about those despicable Leafs. To my surprise she said, "I'm a Howey and my father was Mel Howey. He was your uncle's best friend." She continued, "A few years ago, I was helping my family sort through some of his belongings, and we came across a folder of letters that were written by your uncle to him during the war." I was speechless – there were letters written by my uncle?? In his own handwriting?? During the war??

Yes, she said. I asked if I could see the letters and she said certainly. I explained to her that I was only in town for one more day – could I come and pick the letters up and have them copied? I promised to have it done professionally, and that I would treat the letters very carefully. She said no problem and offered to bring the letters to my father's house the next day.

True to her word, Mel's daughter came to my father's house the next day with the letters. I invited her in and again promised that I would take care of the letters and return them promptly after I had them copied. She replied, "You know, these letters were written by your uncle, and we have read them. Why don't you keep them?" I was quite taken by her generosity and thanked her profusely.

I now had in my possession a direct connection to my uncle, my namesake, in his own handwriting. I could seriously begin to understand this person who sacrificed his life and left me his name. I immediately read all of Donald's letters, which were addressed to his best friend Mel. The first one was written on December 7, 1942, while both were in training in southern

Ontario. The last letter was written on November 18, 1943, one week before Donald's first, and only mission. I wanted to share the contents with my father and ask him more questions about my uncle, but he had just said goodbye to his wife, my mother, and I could not bring myself to interfere with the family's bereavement at that time.

Over the years, I often wondered what could I do with the letters. There were sixteen letters, many quite short and terse, and certainly not enough material to support a manuscript about him. As I continually contemplated Shakespeare's phrase, "what's in a name," there was much more of my uncle's story that I needed to uncover. I began to accumulate a broad array of genealogical records, newspaper articles, and government files. I was slowly able to compile a record of his heritage, his life, and his service. Finally, as most of us occasionally do, in 2012 I googled myself to find out what information was on the Internet about me. To my astonishment, deep into my search, I came across a tribute to my Uncle Donald on a website called InMemory,[1] maintained by Pierre Vandervelden of Belgium. There in front of me was a picture of my uncle's gravestone in a cemetery in Carignan, France. I had stumbled across my uncle's final resting place while looking for myself! It was incredulous.

Beneath my uncle's memorial was the instruction: "if you want a king-size copy of this picture, please e-mail me." I immediately emailed Pierre and explained to him that this was my namesake uncle, and I had no knowledge that he was buried in this location. Pierre explained to me that he often leads a group of individuals who go to small cemeteries in France and Belgium to take photographs and document members of the Allied Forces who were buried there. Most people, he said, knew and visited the largest and most famous cemeteries. His goal was to bring attention to the smaller, less well-known sites and honour the soldiers laid to rest there. In his own words, "God bless them all. May they always remain in our memories." Pierre sent me a high-resolution photo.

I immediately felt that I had to attend the gravesite. Having spent a fair amount of time in Europe, I was very comfortable travelling abroad. I had visited Paris on numerous occasions, and I had spent ten years studying French as a second language in Canada. I had even spent a couple of weeks studying French in Chambury, France, and by that time I was comfortable in a conversation held at a relaxed pace. However, my language experience had been a decade ago. Since that time, I had started an education program in Central America, and I switched to studying Spanish. Unfortunately, (or probably, fortunately) I have a mathematical brain. Managing to keep two foreign languages up to speed was definitely not within my capabilities. I had been to France in the past year and struggled tremendously with the language. Every time I tried to speak in French, Spanish words would come to mind, and I would muddle and fuddle about awkwardly. I wanted to have a positive experience visiting my uncle's final resting place and hopefully speak to some Carignan residents and thank them for maintaining my uncle's grave. I contacted my good friend Pierre Lauginie, who lived in Paris, and asked if he would accompany me on my journey. Pierre responded immediately: *Bien Sur!! Je n'ai connais pas que ton oncle était un héros de la guerre!*

It was late fall 2012 and, in the spring of 2013, I had a commitment to attend a conference in Poland. I began to make my travel arrangements. It was not an easy task. At that time, I was running an education program for pre-service teachers in rural Costa Rica. Each year I would spend six weeks at an environmental school, Colegio Ambientalista Isaiah Retana Arias in Pedrogoso, near San Isidro. I was committed to this program until the first of May, and I had to be in Poland shortly afterwards, then back home to begin another project. However, it didn't matter about the challenge, the miles or even the expense; I was not going to bypass this experience.

I travelled to Costa Rica in the spring of 2013, continuing with the program I had been involved in for many years. I took twelve university students, pre-service teachers, to Costa Rica each year to teach in an rural environmental school and live in the community. The students were typically young women, very talented and conscientious, who always looked forward to their experiences, and to being immersed in the community with a local Spanish speaking family.

In the Costa Rica program, I spent a great deal of time with my students, teaching them Spanish for eight months, preparing an array of environmental lessons in Spanish, and practicing in school settings for several months before proceeding to Costa Rica. It was a unique challenge for them to go from never speaking Spanish to teaching in Spanish in just eight months. Typically, most of the students were initially quite nervous about beginning their experience. It was a joy to watch them as they confronted these challenges and emerged from their practice with a great deal of skill and confidence. By the end of the program, they often spoke of their personal journeys and the growth and maturity they had gained.

It was now 2013 and I was about to depart on my own personal journey. I had to leave the school and students a few days before the program ended, so I met with the group and discussed our progress and what it meant to them. They talked about their experiences, the language, the culture, teaching, and their relationships with their students, and especially their Spanish speaking homestay families. They asked where I was going, and I told them I was also going on a personal adventure:

to visit the grave of my namesake uncle. We talked of personal challenges, hills to climb, and how "getting there" - advancing to new level of understanding - was half the fun. It now seemed as if I was the student, but it made me feel ready.

Early the next day, I packed my belongings and left my homestay to begin a long and arduous journey from Costa Rica to Carignan, France. I put on my backpack and started what was always the most difficult task in my Costa Rican experience: walking up the long steep hill where I stayed, with a full backpack. Every year it seemed to get harder, and I convinced myself the only way to conquer this task was one step at a time. It was seven a.m., already warm in Costa Rica, and I was in a full sweat by the time I reached the road. I took off my backpack and sat by the side of the road for a few minutes, laughing at myself. *It is all downhill from here*, I thought. Thinking of my students' experiences, and the hills they had climbed, it appeared that in my journey, I would soon arrive at a goal that had been on my mind for more than fifty years.

I walked one more kilometre to school, where I said my final goodbyes to staff and students. The morning bell for recreo rang, and the students and staff emptied into the halls. One thing about the school's halls is that there was a roof to protect you from the rain, but no walls, and you could pretty much see across the entire school. Three of my students were walking down the opposite hall and waved. I returned the wave, gave a thumbs up, grabbed my backpack, and headed for the road to catch a taxi to town.

My actual journey to my uncle's gravesite was unique. My wife and son had joined me in Costa Rica for a couple of weeks. Together, on the 16th of April, we started with the hike to school with our backpacks, next a twenty-minute taxi ride from school to town, then a three-hour bus ride to San Jose, and another twenty-minute taxi ride to the hostel. When I travel with my students, we stay in a hostel both coming and going, and I have come to know the owners, who offered to drive us to the airport in the morning. The next day we flew from San Jose to Toronto, where my wife and son boarded a flight for home. I stayed the night and boarded a plane to Paris, and then on to Warsaw. I arrived in Warsaw on the 18th and took another three-hour bus ride to my destination at Torun, Poland. After my work at Torun, there was a three-hour bus ride back to Warsaw, an overnight in Warsaw, and a flight back to Paris. It was an exhausting trip, but I was reminded of my students, who had faced many issues yet emerged in a better place, ready to take on new adventures. I was ready, my undivided attention turned to my trip to Carignan and my Uncle's final resting place.

Footnotes Chapter 11

[1] InMemory, http://www.inmemories.com/index.htm

Chapter 12

Carignan

So today, we can tell them: they wrote a beautiful story.

– Denis Lourdelet

Paris is such a wonderful place to visit in the spring. The talented American jazz singer, Ella Fitzgerald, loved Paris "every moment of the year," but I would like to point out that she mentioned springtime first. The season is very beautiful, not too warm, and the crowds are manageable. The trees are starting to bloom, and carefully manicured gardens are awash in colour. A stroll through the street markets or along the Seine is a grand pleasure in the afternoon. It is always exciting to be in Paris, but on this occasion, I felt special. My work was behind me, and my excitement grew as I realized that I was nearing my destination: a place completely unfamiliar to me in my lifetime, but a meaningful personal experience.

I booked a room at the hotel Ibis, near Gare du Nord, and made my way there from the airport. I have been to Paris on multiple occasions and have visited all the major sites, but I did give myself an extra day to take in "Les Invalides." It seemed appropriate for my trip. L'Hôpital des Invalides is a complex breakfast. I had arranged to meet my friend Pierre, who was accompanying me to Carignan, at the train station. We never really agreed on a specific location; we just met each other wandering aimlessly through the foyer. As our eyes made contact, a smile could instantly be found on both of our faces. We had not seen each other in quite a while, and it was wonderful to meet again. Pierre is a historian of science, and you can talk to him endlessly about French contributions to the development of electricity. He was an expert on Coulomb, Ampere, and many other scientists, both well-known or obscure. You could always find their work and contributions to science enthusiastically explained by Pierre, usually in the guise of a captivating story.

Pierre had already purchased our train tickets to Sedan, so we made our way to the platform and waited for a short while to board the train. As we settled on board, Pierre took out a folder that contained a wide range of notes and information about my uncle, his plane, and the circumstances of his demise. Although I had already found most of this information, it was a kind gesture on Pierre's part to spend so much of his time preparing for my visit. Pierre had contacted the mayor of Carignan and members of the local Historical Society in the Ardennes region. He provided me with their correspondence and the arrangements they had made for me the next day. It was a pleasure to have a friend who went to such lengths to make my visit most meaningful. The French clearly had strong feelings towards the Allied Forces that helped liberate France. My uncle was seen and referred to, on many occasions in the next few days, as a hero. Numerous individuals went to great lengths to ensure that my visit was the best I could experience.

Pierre and I arrived in Sedan in the late afternoon and made our way to our hotel, where we spent the night discussing our latest work. Sedan is a small city of about 20,000 persons in northeast France, at the crossing of the Meuse River. It can be found about ten kilometres from the Belgian border, on the edge of the rolling hills in the Ardennes region. Sedan is a peaceful, well-kept city, with pleasant streets lined with shops, restaurants, and creative architecture. However, the beauty of Sedan has not been without disruption; its history has been marked with periods of intense hostilities. The crossing of the Meuse River was always a lure for invading armies, and many battles took place in the region. During the Second World War, the German army was engaged in a serious conflict with the French in the Battle of Sedan. The constant air raids of the Luftwaffe were intense and destructive, destroying many of the houses in the town. The invading forces marched through the town in victory and Sedan remained occupied for four years. Young Stanislas Greb, who witnessed the crash scene of Donald's plane in 1943, knew and suffered through the dangers that occupied his community for many years.

Sedan, founded in the fifteenth century, is also well known for its medieval castle. If you watched the Netflix classic series *Les Misérables* you will have seen the castle in many of the scenes. Surrounded by a gigantic moat, Pierre and I enjoyed a leisurely stroll through the ancient towers and tunnels where we were periodically entertained by wandering minstrels, knights, and lords of the castle.

Following a peaceful early morning visit, we took a taxi to get the bus to Carignan. Pierre explained to the taxi driver the purpose of my visit, and the driver, on behalf of his fellow citizens he said, sincerely expressed his thanks for my uncle's sacrifice. He refused my tip. We boarded the bus to Carignan, and along the way a road sign caught my attention – METZ 84 km. The previous day, I had been directed down the Corridor de Metz at the museum, and now I find another sign as if it was reaching out to me. We all know that METZ is a vibrant city in the Lorraine region of France, but I could not help but think that the symbols were meant for me.

Upon our arrival in Carignan, we were met by MM. Raymond and Guien, representatives of the *Cercle Historique et Artistique Yvoisien* (CHAY, a local historical society), who accompanied us to the city hall. At city hall we were welcomed by the Deputy Mayor Michel Doppler, who led us to the council chambers where Nadjia Lahlou, the English teacher in the town's high school, and her husband waited for us. Nadjia provided the translation services for our meeting. We were welcomed heartily and presented with a beautiful paperweight with the city's symbol engraved on one side.

Monsieur Doppler noted that mayor Denis Lourdelet was out of town, but he sent his greetings, and left a speech that he made at a ceremony celebrated between the Ardennes-Canada partnership and the city of Carignan. He explained that every year a remembrance ceremony takes place in various cemeteries around the Ardennes region to honour the Allied Forces who lost their lives in the war. At this gathering, the country flags of the respective airmen are honoured, and the national anthems are sung with reverence. The Ardennes-Canada Association dedicates this service "to the heroes who helped us by their sacrifice to find peace in France and in the world." The ceremony was held in Carignan, the year previous to my visit, in memory of the five Canadian and two British aviators who lost their lives on Mount Tilleul during the early morning of the 26th of November, 1943. Regrets were passed on that the city was unaware of my interest in visiting my uncle's gravesite at that time. The mayor's speech from that service was read aloud and translated at the meeting for me. The mayor, speaking to a crowd gathered at the cemetery, reflected on the airmen's passing:

> *It's important to underline that these men's death was not in vain, for these air missions prepared for D-Day on June 6th, 1944, which was a turning point during the war.[2]*

The mayor's speech that day was given at the cemetery where the graves are maintained by the city and flowered every year on All Saints' Day. He spoke of remembrance:

> *These seven soldiers sacrificed themselves in order to let us live in a free country. Indeed, this ceremony had to take place because it makes us all remember. This ceremony is, above all, one of collective memory.[3]*

The mayor concluded:

> *These seven men didn't die for nothing. They helped us reclaim our precious freedom in the most generous way. I'd like to dedicate a quotation from Raymond Caron to them. He said: "Ce sont les hommes qui écrivent l'histoire mais ils ne savent pas l'histoire qu'ils écrivent," meaning "These are the men who write history, but they don't know the story they write." So today, we can tell them: they wrote a beautiful story.[4]*

The mayor, in his speech, also reminded everyone that the youngest among us are also affected by these events through the experiences of their parents and grandparents. The more senior members of a family are the ones who remembered the soldiers dying on the front, the resistance, the camps, and the rationing. Indeed, not unlike Donald's life being a byproduct of his grandparents exodus to Canada, fleeing war and famine. In turn, my duty is to remember and pass on this knowledge to my children and grandchildren in the hope that they reflect on the nature and protection of their own freedom.

As we continued with our gathering at the town hall, several accounts of the crash were read aloud and translated for me. One witness, who now lived in Nancy, France, was too frail to travel to meet me, so he wrote a letter. I felt a caring demeanour in his story. After the speeches were read and kind words and thanks were exchanged, M. Doppler asked if I would like to visit the gravesite. We concluded our meeting in the council chambers, and the group escorted me to the cemetery, which was only a few minutes away.

The cemetery was tucked away on the outskirts of the village, surrounded by a gentle rolling countryside so commonly found in the rural regions of France. The headstone markers varied from simple flat crosses to upright monuments etched in modern granite with personalized memorials, cut in stone to last forever.

Gravel paths led around the gravesites, and most of the sites were dotted with fresh flowers. Near the back, three simple markers were emblazoned with the emblems of the Royal Canadian Air Force. The markers were unusual in that they stood side by side within an area marked by a small concrete curb bordering the gravel surface. Flowers lay in the center of the site. After several years of trying to find this small, final resting place for my uncle, I had finally arrived. My destination was not a final ending, but a new beginning to a lifelong journey to get to know my uncle.

The communal graves of Willys Roland Bloch, Earl Allen Burton, Donald Allan Hogg, Peter Thompson McCallum, Victor Wallace McGray, Donald James Metz, and Timothy Wainwright.

My companions were led by the deputy mayor of Carignan, M. Doppler, who asked for a moment of silence as I stood quietly by the communal grave. I looked at the inscription; I read my name, D.J. Metz, 26th November 1943, Age 19. *Just a teenager*, I thought. I recalled his picture with Alex arriving at Bournemouth, and I remembered reading the letters to his best friend Mel. He always wanted to meet up with Mel for a few beers, cards, and laughter; chasing girls, consoling them, writing them letters but never dancing with them. I remembered his love of hockey, his dog Duke, and above all, his love for his mother, my grandmother. Like many others of the baby boom generation born in the postwar years, I carried the name of a close relative who sacrificed their life in the name of the freedom that we enjoy today. In the last few weeks, it meant that I was able to easily move through the countries of Central America, United States, Canada, France, and Poland, while enjoying immensely the diversity and culture each visit brought me. I was truly thankful for this moment.

It took me over sixty years to find that the name on this gravestone was indeed mine. In fact, for most of those years I had no idea that the grave even existed. Yet now, on a beautiful day in spring, amid the rolling green countryside of France, I paused and reflected on my journey. I had started to fill the void that had been within me my entire life. The name on the gravestone was mine, but the grave was not mine. I was alive and thankful for the gratifying day, my new friends beside me, and the picturesque countryside where my uncle had been laid to rest more than seventy years ago.

Like a number of other Canadian boys, I had been given a relative's name after he died in World War II. I never knew him and his life. Brief as his life was, it was rarely discussed in our household. I never knew his physical characteristics, his mood, the significant moments in his life, his favourite things, his personality, his dreams, or his desires. I knew little about his service to our country, nor about his ultimate demise and final resting place. For this young precocious lad, it left a gap that followed me through my years. I often returned to that divide, wondering periodically what it was like to be the man whose name I was chosen to carry. At times, it seemed more like a burden than an honour. On that sunny spring day in France, that burden was lifted, and I could not help but recall the words of the great writer Mark Twain, who said that "you live as long as someone holds a memory of you." I now felt it had become my duty to create that memory and to pass it on.

After a few moments of silence at the grave, and some conversation and accolades from the group, M. Doppler asked if I would like to visit the crash site. The crash site: the place where my uncle's plane had come down in flames, where their bodies were found, unidentifiable. It seemed surreal to me that where my uncle tragically died, I could walk in peace.

La Terre Rouge. The Linden Tree is near the top, slightly right of center.

The crash site was on the hillside close to the cemetery; you could see it from my uncle's grave. We walked up to the hill together, passing through a farm gate as some cows grazed serenely nearby. At the top of the hill named Mont Tilleul, we had a beautiful view of the countryside surrounding Carignan and the town below. I was informed that the crash site was well known, as the plane's remnants remained on the hillside for many years following the war. The location was marked by a solitary Linden tree within a surrounding forest. One member of the group noted how strange this was, as Linden trees were not native to the area. For me it seemed even more peculiar. I am also an amateur musician, and I played mandocello in the Winnipeg Mandolin Orchestra for many years. A few years ago, our orchestra auditioned for a role in Guy Maddin's movie *The Saddest Music in The World*. Our selection for the audition was an orchestral number by Pavel Kulikov, called "The Linden Tree." The piece is a haunting melody some may be familiar with from the movie *The Grand Budapest Hotel*. Maddin loved the piece, and we were cast in the movie.[5]

I mentioned how coincidental this was to our group, and sometime later I came across another song by Franz Schubert. Schubert's exposition *Winterreise*, written in 1827, describes a traveler on a journey, and his number *Der Lindenbaum (The Linden Tree)* reflects on the dreams and memories one may have while resting beneath the branches of a Linden tree. His words appeared to describe my own journey to Carignan.

> *But then the trumpet sounded*
> *And love was not to be.*
> *The call to death or glory*
> *Took you away from me.*
> *You thought that you would never die*
> *For soldiers never see.*
> *But we will never meet again*
> *Beneath the linden tree, beneath the linden tree.*
> *And now I lay my flowers*
> *Beside the linden tree*

Standing on the hill where my uncle died was an emotional experience for me that is most difficult to describe. It remains without doubt that the Linden tree will be a lasting memory I will carry forever.

As our group stood on "La Terre Rouge," we discussed various aspects of the plane crash, the direction of the plane, the flight path between Leeming and Frankfurt, the children who played in the remnants following the war, and the reaction of the community yesterday, today, and tomorrow. After some time, we headed back to city hall at a nice leisurely pace to share a drink as a "glass of friendship." The final act of my hosts was the presentation to me of parts of the plane they had recovered from the crash site. Before I came to Carignan, the members of the local historical society had taken metal detectors up to the crash site to find these vestiges to give me as a remembrance of my day. I will never forget their thoughtfulness, their kindness, and their respect for my uncle. They are truly a kind community.

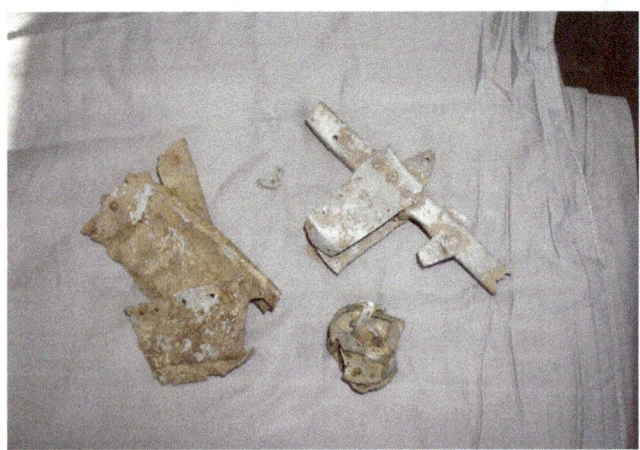

Pieces of the wreckage of Donald's Halifax JD325 airplane

Footnotes Chapter 12

[1] David Wilson, "Was Napoleon Evil?", *The Globe and Mail*, July 13, 2002.

[2] Denis Lourdelet, speech given at Ardennes-Canada memorial service, July 14, 2012.

[3] Denis Lourdelet, speech given at Ardennes-Canada memorial service, July 14, 2012.

4 Denis Lourdelet, speech given at Ardennes-Canada memorial service, July 14, 2012.

[5] If you are familiar with Maddin's work, you will know it is a bizarre story of a contest during the Depression era to find the saddest music in the world. Roger Ebert gave it 3.5 out of 4 stars. My favourite scene was one with star actress Isabella Rossellini who, with glass legs filled with beer, judges the musicians. I was the Albanian mandolin player at the side of the stage.

Chapter 13

War, What Is It Good For?

The secret of freedom lies in educating people, whereas the secret of tyranny is in keeping them ignorant.

– Maximilien Robespierre

Every November 11, we gather around the local Cenotaph to give thanks to the veterans who gave their lives for us to live in a free and democratic society. The Cenotaph represents those who are buried elsewhere and we lay wreaths to honour their service. We mark the occasion with the saying *"Lest We Forget."* As a child whose name was called on that day, I often contemplate "what is it that we do not want to forget?" I wonder what it is that people who sacrificed their lives, their families, or who lived through the tragedies and atrocities of war want us to remember? What do they want to remember?

In his work, *War Is A Force That Gives Us Meaning*, Chris Hedges tells the story of Ljiljana, a Bosnian woman caught in the conflict with Serbia in the 1990s. During the war, Ljiljana, once young and beautiful, now toiled through the day. Her hair was dry and brittle, her cheeks were hollow, and her teeth decayed. Ljiljana and her friends had become emaciated, living in distress and fear of snipers on the rooftops. She had lost her family, and in the aftermath of the war was fortunate enough to emigrate to Australia. Ljiljana told Hedges, a few days after she was forced to identify the body of her father:

> *I will marry a man who has never heard of this war and raise children who will be told nothing about it, nothing about the country I am from.*[1]

Today we watch thousands of Ljiljanas flee their homeland in Ukraine as Putin's Russia brutally bombs civilian locales such as hospitals, refugee centers, and train stations. Their stories, like those of Ljiljana and so many other innocent victims of war, are devastatingly sad. It is so easy to see how they are justified in their desire to forget, to move on, and to raise their children outside of the cruelty and atrocities of war.

The desire to forget and leave behind the vile memories of war is not new. Across many families, dialog of the war, and of the contribution and sacrifice of family members, is not always common. Just losing a son, a daughter, a brother, or a sister in these circumstances was tragic enough for the family. Life had to go on. Many others share similar experiences. The songwriter James Gates notes that his grandfather did not talk about his military service with him at all, and rarely discussed it with other family members. It was only after his grandfather passed away that he came into possession of his pilot's logbook. Finally, he was able to "reconcile the man he knew with the man he read about in those logs."[2] Gates then wrote the song "*Keep it in the Sky*" to celebrate his grandfather.

It is not hard to understand why people, especially ones so cruelly affected by war, have little desire to recount the details of their horror. Still, we gather as we should, once a year, to honour those who gave their lives so we can live ours in peace. We lay a wreath out of respect for the fallen, and we honour those who fought and survived. On this special day, November 11, the focus is on those who served, as it must be. However, for the rest of the year, we tend to avoid discussion of their service, the suffering of the innocent, and our family losses. No doubt, in time, our memories will leave behind the current tragedies of Ukraine.

Even though, from time to time, if we recall these periods of war, we rarely ponder the roots of war and oppression that exist in our very being. I would argue that this discussion should become a cornerstone to our understanding of the world, and that we owe this understanding to those who served and gave us peace. The better all of us comprehend the paths that lead us to war, the more committed we are to honouring those who gave their lives to ensure our freedom. Most importantly, it is this understanding that may alert us and help to prevent the rise of future oppressive regimes.

But what exactly is it that we should remember? What do we owe the Donalds of the world? It is a sad reflection on humanity that so many lives are defined and determined by war. How does a teenager like my uncle, full of life and energy, take his final breath as a consequence of dropping bombs on his ancestral home? What set of circumstances leads one to suffer such an untimely and tragic ending?

Human conflict cuts across centuries of time, and as we live and grow the framework for our lives, we tend to leave behind the foundations of our being. We do not seem to be aware that our culture, and the norms that influence us, are established well before we arrive in this world.

I am presently a retired Canadian baby boomer who, like most of my generation and subsequent generations, has little experience with war or war zones outside of what we watch on the evening news. In my travels as a teenager in the late 1960s and early 1970s, I was in contact with a number of American draft dodgers. They fled their country to avoid the draft in the United States for service in Vietnam. Riots were common in the USA at that time, and I sympathized with these young men who left their home and families during a questionable war that destroyed the lives of millions at home and abroad. I picked up the mantra with Country Joe and the Fish, who sang at the iconic Woodstock festival in 1969, "*One, two three, four, what are we fighting for?*" A year later, Edwin Starr's "*War (What is it Good For?)*" resonated powerfully with me and these young Americans. Yet the United States fought on in Vietnam. Even as American casualties and opposition to the war grew, many Americans remained unwaveringly dedicated to their armed forces. I once had an American friend who was enjoying some adventures in Canada when he was drafted into service. He decided to go home. I asked him, "Why return, just stay in Canada and dodge the draft." He was close with his family, and his reply was that his family would be more proud of a dead soldier than a living draft dodger. He went home.

What drives us to embrace this passion for war? What are the forces that place war as a cornerstone of our existence even when there are unbearable costs in human lives, pointless societal upheavals, and dismal economic collapse? Why is the world continually at war? In the 20th century alone, over 100 million persons have died in war. Currently, over 20 million serve in military service around the world. It is estimated that over 75 million, or roughly three percent of the world's population, died in World War II as the result of military and civilian casualties, as well as disease and starvation in the civilian population.[3] Later in the Vietnam War, over 50,000 American soldiers lost their lives, and the Americans inflicted death and destruction, ten to twenty times their own losses, on the Vietnamese.

Ironically, there is generally widespread support within a country at the beginning of a war. However, as casualties mount, support for the conflict decreases rapidly. It is not surprising, since civilians often endure suffering as much as armies do in war zones. They are shot, bombed, raped, starved, and driven from their homes. Refugees often number in the tens of millions,[4] and they have high mortality rates due to disease and dangers such as ocean crossings. Refugees are often rejected at border crossings, and if they manage to get asylum in another country, they are treated as second-class citizens or a foe. Children also suffer tremendously from war. Some are forced into fighting wars as child soldiers, they lose limbs and contract deadly diseases; others may be channeled into prostitution. Women also bear additional burdens as they must assume a larger economic role in wartime. In the cruelest of circumstances, such as Ljiljana's case, they are impelled to forage for food, water, and medicine to keep their families alive.

In its darkest moments, war leads to genocide. According to the United Nations, genocide is the act "to destroy, in whole or in part, a national, ethnic, racial or religious group."[5] Most of us are familiar with the Jewish Holocaust as an act of genocide, yet many other genocides have been committed, or attempted, in recent times – including in Cambodia, Iraq, Bosnia, and Rwanda. Canadian General Romeo Dallaire was in command of the UN peacekeeping mission during the genocide committed involving the Tutsis and Hutus in Rwanda. He repeatedly tried to warn the UN Security Council about the impending disaster, but the response was always "You will not intervene."[6] As the current war in Ukraine evolves, memories of "genocidal" tactics used by Stalin in the 1930s are being summoned by the illegal Russian invasion.[7] Additionally, the International Criminal Court (ICC) recently issued a warrant for the arrest of Russia's President Vladimir Putin for the unlawful deportation and transfer of Ukrainian children to Russia. It never ends.

So, why do we fight? Some have argued that it is genetic. Others have suggested that it is noble. Some even consider war to be a necessary attribute of a peaceful society. The American Civil War, while devastating in terms of loss of life, is still considered by some as the means by which the United States emerged as a strong and resilient country. In the final scene of his documentary *The Civil War*, Ken Burns shows Union and Confederate soldiers shaking hands at a reunion seventy-five years later in a reflection of this American unity. Others, of course, would argue differently. It is somewhat ironic to see a lack of diversity portrayed in this final act of unity.

Ian Morris, an historian, argues war is what makes the world safer. That is, the only way to govern large populations is with strong governments. He states that:

The men who ran these governments cracked down on killing not because they were saints, but because well-behaved subjects were easier to govern and tax than angry, murderous ones. States that suppressed violence within their borders tended to grow; those that did not, tended to fail.[8]

Morris' answer to Edwin Starr's insightful question – "War, What is it Good For?" – seems to be that war produces autocratic governments, which make the world a safer place. At the heart of his argument is the fact that the percentage of deaths caused by war in our times is considerably lower than in ancient times. In other words, our risk of dying by war today is about one-tenth the risk than if you lived during the Stone Age. In absolute terms, it seems that hundreds of millions of lives lost to war are ok because there are still lots of us left. Peaceful progress in civilization seems irrelevant; we live for war.

Is it futile for us to suggest that there may be a peaceful way forward? Hedges points out that in the last 3,400 years of humankind we have experienced just 268 years of peace. If the loss of human lives is not enough to motivate us, a clear understanding of the business of war might open some eyes.

Wars are tremendously costly. Since 1975, the United States has spent between 3 and 6 percent of its GDP on defense. This amount, now approaching $800 billion per year, is 15 to 30 percent of the entire federal budget. In comparison, the annual spending on education is $70 billion. Between 1940 and 1996 the USA spent over $19 trillion on the military, compared to $1.7 trillion on health care.[9] In the most recent budget, March 2022, the USA spent almost 50 percent on military related expenses.[10] In the face of such exorbitant costs, what does drive us to war? One cogent argument is greed, and the existence of the military industrial complex in some form or another.

The military industrial complex (MIC) is a term coined by American President Dwight Eisenhower in his farewell speech of 1961. The MIC consists of the effective policies and fiscal relationship between the government and the arms industry. Eisenhower, recognizing the potential for corruption in this relationship, warned:

The potential for the disastrous rise of misplaced power exists and will persist. We must never let the weight of this combination endanger our liberties or democratic processes. We should take nothing for granted. Only an alert and knowledgeable citizenry can compel the proper meshing of the huge industrial and military machinery.[11]

Eisenhower's appeal for an alert and knowledgeable citizenry is prescient, given that Ike himself was a military general. This "machinery" includes political contributions and lobbying of legislators to influence the awarding of contracts and the distribution of money. These often sketchy allocations provide support and significant profits for corporations such as Lockheed and Boeing, to name only two.[12] Significant funds can also be directed to "independent contractors," military companies such as Blackwater Security Consulting (later called XE Services and then Academi).

These expenditures appear to be a direct contradiction of Eisenhower's cogent warning. Blackwater, incorporated in 1997, received about $735,000 from the USA budget; by 2005 this amount increased to $25 million, and a year later it reached $600 million.[13] There is no question that war is "good" for them – the management and shareholders of these companies – while the average person reaps nothing. Moreover, especially for many third world countries on the receiving end of these weapons, the return is usually more tragedy, death, and destruction. But heck, it's better than living in the Stone Age, right? Also, companies from the USA and many other countries export tens of billions of dollars of military equipment every year. Approximately half of USA exports go to developing countries, keeping them in relentless turmoil and Americans employed. Ironically, over time, American troops often come up against their own weaponry.

A further absurdity exists as war is constantly waged. We not only exercise our brawn, but we employ a wide swath of our brain power as war increasingly becomes a technological battle. The challenge is in who can build the better tank, or who is capable of designing the fastest bomber or drone. Measures and countermeasures expand like video games. The World War II air war my uncle fought in is an excellent example. One battle of the brains which started to emerge during this conflict was the development of radar detecting and radar scrambling devices. To confuse radar detection, bomber crews, like Donald's, would drop aluminum chaff called "window" from their plane to deflect signals and blur radar devices. On the enemy's radar screen, it would look like thousands of tiny blips, increasing the difficulty in locating the aircraft. In response, German scientists recognized that the chaff changed speed differently than the aircraft from which they were released. By measuring the relevant Doppler shift, the defense systems were able to differentiate the reflected signal of the aluminum from that of the target plane. The science is brilliant. I spent a significant part of my life as a physics teacher; I taught about the Doppler shift without ever contemplating that it was used to locate and destroy my uncle's plane.

"Window," and the Doppler effect, is just one example of the way we use our intellect to develop or counter an advantage in war. In the nuclear age, we must pay attention to Chris Hedges' assertion that "modern industrial warfare may well be leading us, with each technological advance, a step closer to our own annihilation." A popular quote, often attributed to physicist Albert Einstein, supports Hedges' view: "I do not know with what weapons World War III will be fought, but World War IV will be fought with sticks and stones."[14]

War, certainly in the 20th century, also has a wide array of negative effects on the home front, even in peaceful times. Heidi Peltier,[15] an assistant research professor at the University of Massachusetts, argues that while federal spending in military, defense and other related industries produces elevated levels of employment, spending that money in other areas such as health, education, and sustainability endeavours would result in far more jobs; a phenomenon she calls "an opportunity cost." There are also other ramifications of out-of-control military spending in our immediate lives. In recent years, in the wake of protests of the brutal murders of George Floyd and Breonna Taylor, Jessica Katzenstein, a post-doctoral scholar at Harvard University, writes that "at least fourteen local law enforcement agencies in ten states have received free mine-resistant vehicles built for the USA military."[16] In other words, the war machinery is being turned on their fellow Americans. Thus, war is devastating to civilians, including children who may suffer tremendously. Instead of spending money on developing a civil society, we support a military industrial complex that is rife with corruption and greed, and politicians line their own pockets. So why do we persist? Can you imagine what we could accomplish with the resources spent on the military if they were directed to improving our way of life? But wait, doesn't every country in the world have, and need, a military? Actually no, there is an outlier; - consider Costa Rica – a small country in Central America.

After a disputed election in 1948 led to a civil war in Costa Rica, Jose Figueres emerged as the country's leader. Figueres enacted a wide range of new progressive policies including disbanding and banning the nation's army, granting women the equal right to vote, introducing public education for all, and establishing a new constitutional government. Figueres, citing Roosevelt's programs during the Depression era, called for an International New Deal. Today, Costa Rica remains the most developed region in Central America, avoiding warfare, poverty, and the authoritarianism found in many neighbouring countries. The money saved from the lack of a military, and expenditures on a corrupt military industrial complex, was directed towards the development of an advanced public education system, and an environmental attitude second to none. I worked in schools in Costa Rica for a significant amount of time over a ten-year period, and I always admired the teachers, who considered themselves to be Costa Rica's army. This "army" has produced a literacy rate in Costa Rica equivalent to first world countries like Canada. While Costa Ricans still face many formidable challenges, the people of the country remain among the happiest in the world.[17]

Happiness is certainly a quality that all of us wish to pursue. So, why are so many people so angry? Chris Hedges, a Pulitzer Prize-winning journalist, argues that war is a deadly drug that "dominates culture, distorts memory, corrupts language, and infects everything around it."[18] He argues that many of us have lives that we view as worthless and unfulfilled. Within this void there is an inherent yearning for a nationalist cause that unites us while it diminishes and erases "the anxiety of individual consciousness." Consequently, we circumvent our personal responsibilities as war becomes a distraction and forms its own culture. We become one with our neighbours and our country, and in the face of a common enemy, it gives us a cause, a reason to be noble.[19] While we idolize and grieve our comrades, who are killed by a despicable enemy that lacks humanity, our own killing concerns us little. In Hedges' words, "Our dead. Their dead. They are not the same."[20]

We have seen many examples of this outlook in recent times. While Americans mourned their victims of the 9/11 attack – rightfully so – they remained blind to the years of oppression they inflicted upon other countries in the world. Over the years, with policies, like those that enabled the Iran Contra affair, the Americans have supported an array of dictatorial leaders as they attacked revolutionary movements. The war on communism, exemplified by the Vietnam War era, and the control and exploitation of resources in the Middle East and other locales, are further examples of the suppression of foreign states. In Tom Engelhardt's take on Edwin Starr's "*War (What is it Good For?)*," he reflects on the last fifteen years where the USA has been engaged in permanent warfare in the Middle East:

> *The planet's sole superpower with a military funded and armed like none other and a "defense" budget larger than the next seven countries combined (three times as large as number two spender, China) has managed to accomplish – again, quite literally – absolutely nothing, or perhaps (if a slight rewrite of that classic song were allowed) less than nothing.*[21]

War creates a dichotomy; you are either for me or against me. Our enemies are dehumanized while we consider ourselves the personification of virtuousness. Even if you are for me, but are of the same nationality, colour, or religion as my enemy, you can be oppressed. As Hedges notes, "Each side reduces the other to objects – eventually in the form of corpses."[22] What motivates us to continually fall into such devastation? Maybe there are some benefits to war. We might ask, are all wars bad? Are there good wars?

Surely you must be saying by now: should we have sat idly by and watched Hitler destroy Europe? The answer is clearly no – most of us would consider World War II justifiable.[23] We are often faced with the existential dilemma between a preferred idealistic world and the world we live in. Do we stand by and watch Putin destroy Ukraine – murdering children – or do we take a position against him? There are times when we must ascend the moral high ground and stand up to the brutality and oppression waged against a civil society to defend that society. We must do this to honour those, like my uncle, who have previously fallen to provide freedom for us and to maintain the world that we grew up knowing, especially for our children. The challenge before us is monumental.

I maintain that in order to address this challenge we must start by facing our own frailties. One of our most pronounced misconceptions today is our notion of freedom. In reference to the loss of our soldiers in conflict, it is often said that they laid down their lives heroically to preserve our freedom. We must remember this sacrifice. However, we need to reconcile our understanding of freedom with some of the modern-day claims of freedom.

As we watched the daily news in the middle of a devasting pandemic, it was filled with the rants of "anti-vaxxers" who declared their freedom to choose not to receive a vaccination or wear a mask to prevent the spread of a deadly virus. This in fact was their choice, their freedom. As long as they isolated they brought no harm to others. However, in the face of vaccine requirements, they claimed it was their freedom to do as they pleased openly, without being vaccinated, whether it was entering restaurants, hospitals, or crossing borders. They spouted anti-science rhetoric, used conspiracy theories to justify their protests, and adhered to one of the most offensive notions of freedom. They advocated for their freedom to do harm to others in the public commons. Further, to elevate their status, they waved flags and sang national anthems to bring attention to their "faux" patriotism. This exhibition is not the notion of freedom that my uncle, and our service members, gave their lives to maintain.

Andrée Peel, a World War II female resistance fighter from France, provides us with some insight into her notion of freedom in the face of oppression and war. She says:

By the very act of losing our freedom we were able to understand its meaning. It was not just a word in the dictionary with a basic definition; it was not just the ability to do what one wanted to do. It appeared, suddenly, to those of us who had been deprived of it, as possessed of a far wider significance.[24]

Freedom was not just the ability to do what one wanted to do and when you wanted to do it. Andrée continued reasoning that "Freedom meant, first and foremost, having access to the truth." She described the wartime situation in her community where the media – newspapers – had come under the control of the enemies: the Nazis. The media was now a source of lies and distortion, resulting in "a sickening miasma of mutilated news." I heartily agree with Andrée's view that the essential component of freedom is access to the truth. There are several current and recent events that illustrate an understanding of this tenet of freedom. The Canadian "Freedom Convoy," the influence of social media, the rise of Trumpism in the United States, and the Russian invasion of Ukraine are a few that lie on our doorstep today.

The Canadian "Freedom Convoy" consisted of hundreds of trucks and supporters who rolled up to the federal Parliament buildings in downtown Ottawa in January 2022. Initially, they claimed to protest vaccination mandates, specifically for trucks crossing the Canada–US border. They occupied and clogged the downtown area for over three weeks, harassing residents by blaring their horns incessantly. They repeatedly shouted for their "freedom" and their constitutional rights to be restored. However, they were regularly observed drinking, partying, and barbecuing pigs on a spit. They decorated their vehicles with flags, including upside down Canadian flags, Canadian flags adorned with swastikas, and Confederate and Trump flags. They were filmed dancing on the Tomb of the Unknown Soldier and desecrating the statue of beloved Canadian icon Terry Fox[25]. The protesters harassed local businesses, including a homeless shelter, and shouted racial slurs at employees and security guards.

The convoy was initially presented as a trucker's event, however, it was quickly condemned by the Canadian Trucking Alliance, who claimed that the majority in attendance had no relationship with the trucking industry. In fact, the "freedom" convoy was largely promoted by far-right extremists, many who later faced a wide range of serious criminal charges.

Now, whether to support vaccines or mandates is not the issue I wish to present to you. I would just like you to compare the notions of freedom espoused by Andrée Peel and her compatriots with those of the convoy participants. In Andrée's case, she endured physical torture, sexual abuse, widespread murderous invasions, and post-traumatic stress disorder that lasted her lifetime. Her family, friends and neighbours were murdered. Not to mention the thousands of young men and women, like my uncle, who gave their lives so we could live ours. I am not sure she would agree with the notion of freedom advanced by the participants of the convoy. To make matters even more disturbing, numerous politicians, like the newly-elected leader of the Canadian Conservative party, Pierre Poilievre, jumped aboard this "freedom" train to promote political division and gain populist support to advance their own personal agendas.

Much of this pretention around such views of freedom emerged from the evolution of the Internet in the 21st century. In his interviews with convoy participants, Ian Brown [26] reported that they believed the mainstream media is lying about everything. They were especially convinced that the government and medical system lied about the severity of the pandemic. Consequently, they turned to online sources such as TikTok, YouTube, Twitter, and a host of far-right, conspiracy-laden sources to access their information. Brown highlighted the outrageous beliefs espoused by some of the convoy participants: that Fidel Castro was Justin Trudeau's father, the Clintons were recruiting children for sex trafficking, and Bill Gates was supporting the selective breeding of human beings. These were just a few of the unorthodox views he heard in his interviews.

The current state of the online "media" is, increasingly, a significant problem in terms of access to the truth. Historically, our daily news was disseminated in print and on a few news networks through a "free press." The free press was initially seen as honourable; news anchors like Walter Cronkite were widely admired, and Cronkite himself was considered to be "the most trusted man in America." Over time, cable television increased competition, and niche networks like Fox News emerged to focus on specific messaging, dividing their audience according to limited political views. For their part, as news transitioned to the Internet, media companies initially simply placed their print articles online for people to read. Then, reader commentary sections were added to attract interest, increase viewership, and allow everyone to contribute and engage in a meaningful dialogue. The transition is interesting in the sense that we transitioned from being only readers and listeners to becoming "expert" commentators.

Social media also took advantage of the unique ability of the Internet to connect people, initially as a way to stay in touch with family and friends. As social media companies such as Twitter, Facebook, and YouTube started to monetize their platforms, keeping the user online became a target to increase engagement. It became evident to the media moguls that not only could they connect people to others, but they could also connect people to content. Profits were determined by the number of clicks generated, and social media companies directed their users to "clickbait" in the form of videos, pictures, and influencers.

Meanwhile, many online groups soon became dominated by special interests. Users, uninformed to begin with, began to find consolation and support as "both sides" of an argument fuelled their confirmation biases. In order to increase online activity, algorithms were used to track and direct specific content toward specific individuals. "Suggested For You" links are intended to keep you online for as long as possible. In other words, both sides of an issue were not represented fairly, you are directed towards specific content, which is often rife with misinformation. You can now literally sit side by side with your spouse, addressing the same question on the same platform, and form completely different points of view.

Many more schemes are being developed by social media companies such as impersonation, bots, fake accounts, deepfakes, memes, bait and switch tweets, videos, and chat rooms. All of these can broadcast misinformation, usually directed towards naïve and uninformed readers, or at-risk populations.

In many cases, the hidden intention may be to secure a "donation". Joan Donovan, the research director of the Shorenstein Center on Media, Politics and Public Policy, has written extensively on the impact of "pseudo-anonymous influence operations":

To capture this momentum, companies such as Facebook and Twitter began to rebrand their products as tools for free speech. In this new marketing scheme, social media companies were likened to the digital streets or public square, and their products were framed as synonymous with democracy itself.[27]

Social media platforms advance themselves as purveyors of free speech. Donovan also contends that these companies focus on profits without "any care or plans to mitigate the harmful effects such information has on society as a whole." Additionally, she asserts that we are inundated with a "firehose of unprovable facts." Donovan's solution is knowledge, and she maintains that knowledge is power and the means by which we can achieve justice, fairness, and accountability. Donovan's view illustrates the harm that social media is propagating today. Without question, online groups played a key role in the evolution of the "Freedom Convoy." Ryan Broderick traced the rise of the convoy's movement on social media and showed how it led to a con game:

This pipeline – from physical protest to social media to establishment outlets – is what has helped the convoy evolve from a local standoff into a televised event that can raise millions from supporters thousands of miles away.[28]

As the organizers raised multi-millions of dollars and couched their demands in "pseudo-legal language," they literally used Donovan's "firehose" as their essential instrument. Much of the rhetoric on social media that influenced the convoy, from the role of truckers to their notion of freedom was, indeed, a reflection of their own words – "fake news."

Sound familiar? In today's world, Trump's world, phony news is his mantra. While he decries all reporting that is negative to him as "fake news," his supporting news networks, OAN, Newsmax, Breitbart, and Fox News,[29] have become sources of lies and distortion magnified by social media. Andrée Peel claimed from her experiences in World War II, that when we lose the truth, we lose our freedom. She also reminded us that you cannot fully understand freedom until you have lost it.

Today this is reflected in the cries for "freedom" from many of our politicians. Alberta premier Danielle Smith said she does not wear a poppy for Remembrance Day because "it's been ruined for her". Speaking against vaccinations, Smith declared that these were the actions our brave soldiers fought against and the vaccinated population were like puppets following Hitler into tyranny[30]. Such egregious rhetoric clearly illustrates the lack of understanding of the sacrifice made by our men and women in uniform. Even more disturbing is the fact that individuals like Smith are in positions of power and often just turn their heads while we are losing many legitimate aspects of our freedoms today. An emergence of authoritarian rule, political gerrymandering, absurd practices of banning drag shows, mandating or banning dress codes (such as the hijab) and the revoking of women's reproductive rights and their access to safe medical procedures, are just a few examples of issues that are being cast upon us in our world today. All of these matters are being advanced on the misrepresentation of the truth. In the words of the 18th century French politician, Robespierre: "The secret of freedom lies in educating people, whereas the secret of tyranny is in keeping them ignorant."

The recovery of the truth is what heroic individuals like Peel (remember her torture) fought for, and many others, like my uncle, sacrificed their lives for: to recover it and give it back to us. Let us remember those we have lost, who defended our freedoms, by respecting and understanding their lives and their sacrifices. They are us: our children, our family, our friends, and our neighbours. In my journey to uncover the essence of my namesake uncle, I have become aware that, like so many of his comrades, he was just a normal guy. He was lonely, wanting his friends and his family. He loved and trusted his mother and missed her dearly. He wanted to meet a girl, he gambled and drank too much, and was angry when he couldn't connect with his friends. He was a just a young man, but he still surrendered his life for my freedom. As I reflect on the life and death of my uncle, I ask you to reflect on the lives of your loved ones, of Andrée Peel, of our fallen soldiers, and on the simple notion that when we lose truth, we lose our freedom. If we are going to fight for freedom, let us make sure we understand what freedom really means. Lest we forget.

Footnotes Chapter 13

[1] Christopher Hedges, *War Is A Force That Gives Us Meaning* (Anchor Books, 2003): 6.

[2] Matt Olson, "I Knew Him As Grandpa," Saskatoon Star Phoenix, Nov. 12, 2020: https://thestarphoenix.com/entertainment/music/1112-you-ww2-song

Footnotes cont'd

[3] For a more complete discussion of war casualties and social details see Hedges.

[4] Currently in the Ukraine there are more than 6 million displaced.

[5] "Article II, Convention on the Prevention and Punishment of the Crime of Genocide", *United Nations, Office On Genocide Prevention*, https://www.un.org/en/genocideprevention/,

[6] "Roméo Dallaire Still Bears Psychological Scars 25 Years After the Rwandan Genocide," *The Sunday Edition, CBC Radio One*.

[7] "Ukraine war: Kyiv likens Russian 'genocidal' tactics to Soviet-era 'Holodomor' famine," *Euronews with Reuters, AFP*, November 26, 2022. https://www.euronews.com/2022/11/26/ukraine-war-kyiv-likens-russian-genocidal-tactics-to-soviet-era-holodomor-famine.

[8] Ian Morris,"'War! What is it good for?' More Than You Thought," *Special to CNN*, May 1, 2014:
https://www.cnn.com/2014/05/01/opinion/war-benefits/index.html,

[9] Christopher Hedges, "What Every Person Should Know About War," *New York Times*, July 6, 2003:
https://www.nytimes.com/2003/07/06/books/chapters/what-every-person-should-know-about-war.html.

[10] Greg Hadley, "Congress Approves 2022 Spending Bill for Federal Government, Sends it to Biden's Desk," *Air Force Magazine*, March 10, 2022:
https://www.airforcemag.com/congress-approves-2022-spending-bill-for-federal-government-sends-it-to-bidens-desk/

[11] Farewell address by President Dwight D. Eisenhower, January 17, 1961; Papers of Dwight D. Eisenhower as President, 1953-61, *Eisenhower Library; National Archives and Records Administration*.

[12] For a current list see:
https://en.wikipedia.org/wiki/List_of_defense_contractors

Footnotes cont'd

[13] Kemeroff, Alex, "War For Money: Leading Private Military Companies of the World." Feb. 16, 2018: https://medium.com/smartaim-tech/war-for-money-leading-private-military-companies-of-the-world-eab9f9fe2de8

[14] You can read about the origins of the quote here: https://www.snopes.com/fact-check/einstein-world-war-iv-sticks-stones/

[15] Heidi Peltier, "Job Opportunity Cost of War," *Watson Institute For International and Public Affairs, Brown University*, May 24, 2017: https://watson.brown.edu/costsofwar/files/cow/imce/papers/2017/Job%20Opportunity%20Cost%20of%20War%20-%20HGP%20-%20FINAL.pdf

[16] Jessica Katzenstein, "The Wars Are Here: How the United States' Post-9/11 Wars Helped Militarize U.S. Police Cost of War," *Watson Institute For International and Public Affairs, Brown University*, September 16, 2020: https://watson.brown.edu/costsofwar/papers/2020/wars-are-here-how-united-states-post-911-wars-helped-militarize-us-police.

[17] It's a real thing! Lisa Gale Garrigues, "Why Costa Rica Tops the Happiness Index, How a focus on peace is helping this Central American country top the Happy Planet Index," YES1: https://www.yesmagazine.org/issue/climate-action/2019/01/31/why-costa-rica-tops-the-happiness-index,
Lisa provides a nice explanation of the Happy Planet Index and the importance of peace. We should note that the United States ranked 114th. The New Economics Foundation's Happy Planet Index determined that Costa Rica is the greenest and happiest place in the world. The HPI considers three variables: happiness, ecological footprint, and life expectancy.

[18] Christopher Hedges, *War Is A Force That Gives Us Meaning*, (Anchor Books, 2003): 3.

[19] For a more in-depth discussion, see Hedges.

[20] Hedges, *War is a Force*, 13.

Footnotes cont'd

[21] Tom Engelhardt, "War, What Is It Good For? Absolutely Nothing. And No Kidding, That's the Literal Truth When It Comes to War, American-Style," accessed from TomDispatch.com.

[22] Engelhardt, "War", 21.

[23] Nathaniel Rakich, "Most Americans Agree that WWII Was Justified. Recent Conflicts are More Divisive," June 7, 2019, 538.com.

[24] Peel, Andrée. *Miracles Do Happen.*(Loebertas, 2011).

[25] There are a variety of news reports, for example see: https://www.snopes.com/news/2022/02/17/swastikas-canada-freedom-convoy/

[26] Ian Brown, "They Came. They Idled. They Left. What Have Convoy Protesters Been Doing Since They Went Home?" *The Globe and Mail*, June 4, 2022. https://www.theglobeandmail.com/canada/article-ottawa-convoy-protesters-visit-at-home.

[27] Joan Donovan, "Confronting Misinformation, Trolling for Truth on Social Media: What 1990s Internet Protest Movements Share with Today's Disinformation Campaigns," *Scientific American*, October 12, 2020.

[28] Ryan Broderick, "How Facebook Twisted Canada's Trucker Convoy into an International Movement: A Labyrinth of Facebook Groups and Right-Wing Media," *The Verge*, Feb. 19, 2022.

[29] One simply has to review their 2020 reporting on the false and misleading claims about widespread election fraud.

[30] Don Braid, Calgary Herald, Published May 08, 2023

Acknowledgements

This labour of love has covered many years, and I have many people to thank for their assistance. First my family, especially my spouse, Patricia, for her patience and understanding as I pound the keyboard. I extend a heartful thanks to my friend, Pierre Lauginie from Paris, who accompanied me and facilitated the organization of my trip with the town of Carignan. I would also like to thank my friend and colleague, Phyllis Webster, for her feedback and comma intensives, and the book's editor Louise Sianni, for her review and insightful commentary. Additionally, Ross McDonald provided a solid bass for the final version. The book is well researched, and I believe I've made every effort to provide appropriate citations and recognition. If I have made any errors, I apologize.

I would be remiss not to acknowledge the kind people of Carignan, France, especially Deputy Mayor Michel Doppler for his organization and genial reception; the representatives of the Yvoisien Historical and Artistic Circle (CHAY); MM. Raymond and Guien, for helping to recover parts of my uncle's plane; local educator Nadjia Lahlou for her translation services; and Ardennes-Canada President Chantal Messier, who graciously sent me additional information. It is the people of Carignan who never forgot my uncle. They continue to honour and recognize the contribution of the young men who rest in their presence and they respectfully adorn their graves.

The most important message of thanks is for the children, lest they forget

About The Author

Donald J. Metz was a full professor in the Faculty of Education at the University of Winnipeg. Now retired, he maintains Senior Scholar status at the UW. Don holds a BSc in Physics, and a MEd and PhD in Education.

Don was extensively involved with curriculum development in Canada as the principal writer of the Manitoba Physics program, and as author of multiple teaching resources. He was also highly active in the professional development of pre-service teachers initiating special programs at the Inner-City Science Center located in Niji Mahkwa School in Winnipeg, and at the Colegio Ambientalista in Pedrogoso, Costa Rica. Don, with colleague Laura Sokal, also mentored the UW student group Tomorrow's Educators Building Learning Opportunities (TEBLO) who raised over $27 000 and built a school in Nicaragua in 2013.

Don has published papers in a wide variety of academic journals and he has presented at numerous conferences internationally as an invited speaker. He continues to pursue a wide variety of activities to support education while pursuing his lifelong interests in music and writing. In retirement, Don enjoys an active life with his family in Salmon Arm, British Columbia, Canada.

www.ingramcontent.com/pod-product-compliance
Lightning Source LLC
Chambersburg PA
CBHW070733020526
44118CB00035B/1236